THE BEGINNING OF THE END:
Connections Between Genesis and Revelation

By Dr. Kevin M. Ahrens
BRE, BS, MS, MA, MRE, THD

The Beginning of the End

Copyright © 2021 by Kevin Ahrens

All rights reserved.

Published in the United States by Kevin Ahrens, Sebring, Florida

Unless otherwise noted, Scripture quotations are from the King James Version of the Holy Bible. All emphasis is added by the author.

ISBN: 978-1-7327354-4-6

Editing, interior design, and cover by Pete Ford

First edition

Contents

Introduction | 1

First Great Event | 5
Creation – Denying God's Existence
Second Great Event | 32
The Flood – Violence and Immorality
Third Great Event | 58
Tower of Babel – Globalism and the One World
Fourth Great Event | 91
Sodom's Sin – Gay Agenda
Fifth Great Event | 115
The Patriarchs – Sons of Abraham at War

Endnotes | 136

INTRODUCTION

Today everyone is talking about the second coming of Jesus Christ and it's true. It's going to happen. Jesus is coming soon! The biggest question is, How soon? The movie industry believes in the second coming of Christ. Look at all the apocalyptic movies in our theaters today. The book publishers believe in the second coming of Christ. There are hundreds of books on the who, when, and where of the second coming of Christ. In fact, the second coming of Christ is "big business."

I believe Jesus is coming soon. But I must stress that no one knows the date or hour of His coming. Every year we see more biblical signs being fulfilled. Even God's church is an example of His soon return. I believe the church as a whole is dying and is in a state of decay. The Bible calls this the time of the "Laodicean" or lazy church. The second coming of Jesus is the most anticipated event in human history! He may come before you finish this book.

When people talk about the last days, many times they look at my generation with all its craziness in the decade of the sixties and call it the generation that ruined America.

About the author

It was called the hippie generation, of which I was one. I was a drug-addicted street punk. I grew up on Long Island, New York, in a dysfunctional home, abandoned by my father and raised by an alcoholic and drug-addicted mother.

I was thrown out of Catholic school in the third grade and kicked out of public school at age 16. My mother suffered for years and died at age 39. I was 14 years old and felt totally abandoned. I left home and was homeless on the streets of New York. I lived with friends and made my way selling drugs and stealing anything not nailed down. I was constantly in trouble with the police and authorities. At age 17, I ended up living in a 1947 Ford sedan. I was scared, cold, and all alone. One night I overdosed on LSD and had a "bad trip." In great despair and fear, I called out to God for help.

Walking all alone on the streets, I saw a sign in front of the post office, Uncle Sam saying, "I Want You." At 17 I joined the Navy to see the world. I did see the world. I traveled all over America and Europe. I continued my drug use in the Navy and still felt empty and alone. The Navy made a man out of me, but my pain and memories still haunted me.

Someone in New York gave me a pamphlet called "God's simple plan of salvation." The address on the pamphlet was Norfolk, Virginia, right where I was stationed at the time. I went to a place called Missions to Military and there they shared God's wonderful plan for my life and the gift of salvation.

I accepted Jesus Christ as my personal savior and my life changed completely. I was discharged soon afterward and lived in Missions to Military building and there I studied the Bible and started on my path of discipleship. Soon afterward I surrendered my life to full-time service to God.

I received my high school diploma and then enrolled in Bible college and continued my studies for over a decade. I have two bachelor's degrees, three master's degrees, and a doctorate. God's been good to me and changed my life. I do not believe my generation ruined the entire world, but we were part of the beginning of the end.

Are we living in the "last days"?

I invite you to read 2 Peter 3. The title of this book is *The Beginning of the End*. I believe the first 12 chapters of Genesis give us five clues or glimpses into the "End Times of the World."

I believe these clues or glimpses of the beginning of the end began about 150 years ago. In fact, I believe Genesis gives us a glimpse into the days we are living right now! The last days of God's creative world.

I want to propose to you that the first part of the Book of Genesis shows us the beginning of the end. We will look at the first 12 chapters of Genesis and see how these foundational chapters were given to us as the foundation that our world was to be built upon. Genesis is the book of beginnings. We see the foundational beginning of the world, family, and the nations. We are living with the last generation who is destroying all these foundations.

I believe these 12 chapters of Genesis give us a clue to the time of the second coming of Christ. Remember the words of Jesus who said, "But as the days of Noah were, so shall also the coming of the Son of man be" (Matthew 24:37). We are going to go back and look at the days of Noah from Genesis 1 through 12.

I believe that the Industrial Revolution which started 150 years ago was the beginning sign of the last days. God said it this way in Daniel 12:4: "But thou, O Daniel, shut up the words, and seal the book, even to the time of the end: many shall run to and fro, and knowledge shall be increased." In the last days, they will be going faster than ever before. Daniel also said there will be an increase in education.

One hundred fifty years ago, how did people travel? Horse and buggy. How did they travel in the time of Jesus? Horse and buggy. How did people communicate 150 years ago? Writing a letter. How did they communicate during the time of Jesus? Writing a letter.

Are you telling me that things have not changed in the last two thousand years? There have always been some changes throughout history, but they have not changed drastically as we have recently seen. In fact, in the last 150 years, we have seen an unprecedented change due to the industrial, educational, and scientific revolution. Today, we cannot even keep up with all the new technology.

You go and buy a cell phone and by the time you come home, it is obsolete. Why? Because the Bible says that in the last days there will be an increase in technology and an increase in communication. The Book of Revelation says the antichrist will be able to be seen by every person in the world at the same time. That was impossible until satellites and cell phones. So, my word to you today, my friends, is that it is very, very possible we are living in the "Last Days" that the Bible spoke about. As you read this book you will see five Great Events that have prepared us for the return of Jesus Christ and the end of the world. One by one, our foundations of a civil and spiritual world have been torn down and destroyed. 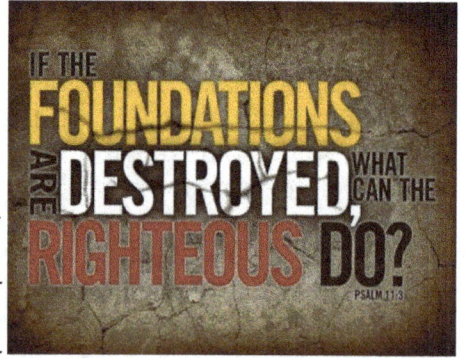 Yes, in our lifetime we are seeing the destruction of everything man and God has built. God help us!

FIRST GREAT EVENT

Creation – Denying God's Existence

I think Genesis is going to answer the question, When will Jesus return and when will be the end of the world? In Matthew 24:3, when Jesus was on the Mount of Olives, the disciples came to Jesus and said, "Tell us, when shall these things be? and what shall be the sign of thy coming, and of the end of the world?" Jesus then gives a discourse for the entire chapter and all of what he speaks about is of our life today. He also spoke of the times of Noah and what was seen then will occur again in the last days.

The entire Bible story really is one story. Someone said *history* is "His Story." Let us take another look at a glimpse into our days, which were spoken of in the Bible.

> This second epistle, beloved, I now write unto you; in both which I stir up your pure minds by way of remembrance: That ye may be mindful of the words which were spoken before by the holy prophets, and of the commandment of us the apostles of the Lord and Saviour: Knowing this first, that there shall come in the last days scoffers, walking after their own lusts, And saying, Where

is the promise of his coming? for since the fathers fell asleep, all things continue as they were *from the beginning of the creation.* – 2 Peter 3:1–4

Peter says if you want to know when the world will end *look* toward the beginning of creation.

But there is more proof. There is so much more. Let us go back to the beginning. Go to Genesis 1. Do you really want to know when I am coming? Look at the beginning of creation. Some people say, "The Bible is so complicated." No, it is not. It is all one story from beginning to end. This is not complicated; it is as easy as ABC.

I hope young people are reading the rest of this chapter. I want to tell you about the biggest lie that has ever been told. What is it? It is the theory of evolution.

I remember hearing a cute story about students in an elementary school. The classroom was filled with young minds and a teacher who was teaching on evolution. The students were not getting any of this silly evolution. The teacher said to Tommy, "Stand up." And Tommy stood up and she said, "Go outside and look around," and he did. He came back in, and she said, "Did you see the trees?" He said, "Yes, ma'am." "Those trees are real. Did you see the grass?" He said, "Yes, ma'am, I did." "Then the grass is real. And did you see all the leaves?" And he said, "Yes. I saw all the leaves." "Then the leaves are real. Did you see God?" He said, "No, I guess God's not real." Little Susie stood up and said, "Can I take the class just for a moment?" Okay. She said, "Tommy, go outside again." He went outside, came back in. "Did you see the trees?" He said, "Yes, I did. "Then the trees are real. Did you see the grass?" "Yes, I did." "Then the grass is real. And when you came back in, did you see the teacher?" "Yes, I did." "Then the teacher is real. Did you see her brain?" "No, I did not." Susie said, "Oh, I guess her brain does not exist!" It does not get any better than that.

When we talk about this thing of creation, what we are really talking about is an event that occurred six thousand years ago. Yes, I said six thousand years ago. Today you are taught in schools and Disney World and the Smithsonian Institute that the world is billions and billions of years old. Or as Carl Sagan, the famous Nova PBS television scientist used to poorly say, "Bollions" of years.

May I begin by telling you of my educational experience? One of my master's degrees is in biology. I also have a bachelor's degree in biology. I have taught science from kindergarten all the way through twelfth grade. So, I speak from personal knowledge. I also hold a Bachelor's, Master's, and Doctorate in biblical studies.

I think it is interesting that the creation of the world had not been disputed for six thousand years. There have been many stories and myths told about creation, but all these stories have a god or gods who were the creators. Only in the last 150 years have we elevated ourselves to think that the whole universe came about by "chance." They want us to believe there was and is no god! As someone said, "Slime + Time = Mankind."

We must believe by faith that the God of the Bible created all the universe. This Judeo-Christian belief of creation, as written in Genesis 1, is the doctrine that most of the world has accepted as truth for over four thousand years of recorded history.

We use an oxymoronic word, "prehistoric." How can we know anything before history? Who was there to record it? Most of the prehistoric science is surmised or is an educated guess based on the scientist bias. Thus, they use any evidence to fit their preconceived theories. If any evidence against evolution is seen or even asked to be studied, it is thrown out or ridiculed.

Any belief before recorded history which has not been seen or experienced is a matter of faith. True science is based on observation. Without observation, we are merely using our imagination to surmise a conclusion.

I believe the world that we live in is six thousand years old. How old? Wait a minute. No way. Yes way. God began the entire universe by using His creative voice and spoke all into existence.

Genesis 1 says that in the beginning, God created the heavens and the earth. He also created Adam and Eve in His own image. He gave mankind the ability to choose between good and evil. Mankind chose evil and sin entered the universe.

Most people today do not want to acknowledge their sin nature. Therefore, people do not want to believe in creation, because if you believe in creation, you must believe in the fall. If you believe in the fall, you must believe in sin. If you believe in sin, then you must believe in a consequence for sin. The biblical consequence of sin is that everybody who sins is going to hell.

That is the real story. Nobody wants to be accountable. God created the world and filled it with life and beauty, but sin corrupted the world. Since the fall of man this world has been dying and will eventually end.

God's timeline

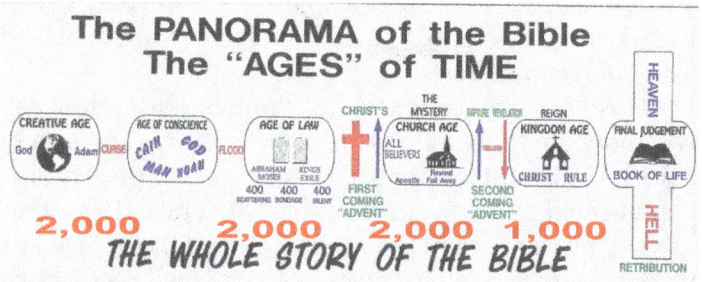

How old is this world and when will it end? From creation to the flood is about two thousand years. From the flood to the time of Christ about two thousand years.

From the time of Christ to today about two thousand years. That is a total of six thousand years. Then Jesus will return, and we will live and reign with Christ for a thousand years, this is called the millennium kingdom. That is now a total of seven thousand years.

2,000+2,000+2,000+1,000=7,000

The Bible says a day with the Lord is a thousand years (2 Peter 3:8). I believe God gave us a clue to the world's age in creation. God created the world in six days and on the seventh day, He rested. Our world has labored about six thousand years and will soon enter a thousand-year period of rest, called the Millennial Kingdom (Revelation 20:1–7).

You may say, "How do you know that, preacher? You were not there. How can you know the actual dates and years?" Well, that is why you must read and study those difficult and tedious books of the Bible, Numbers and Deuteronomy. Someone begat someone who begat somebody who begat somebody and they lived fourscore and so many years. You add it up. Creation has spanned seven thousand years.

Listen, this is not rocket science. What year are we in today? 2020. It has been 2,020 years since the birth of Jesus Christ. Hold that thought just for a moment. Jesus said He was born in the fullness of time. What did He mean? Daniel said that the Jewish nation would rebuild the Temple. At the time of Christ's birth, they were preparing for the Messiah. This is why Anna and Simeon were waiting at the Temple for the promised Messiah. They were told they would see the face of the Messiah. This is a part of the Christmas story. All of Israel was anticipating the coming of Messiah. Daniel said the Messiah would come in 490 years, after the Temple was rebuilt and dedicated. Everyone at that time was living with anticipation of the coming King of the Jews, the Messiah.

Jesus was born 450 years from the date of the Temple dedication. You see, he came to become the King of the Jews. We know that the first Kings who reigned—Saul, David, and Solomon—reigned for forty years each. Jesus was supposed to become the King of the Jews when He turned forty years old, but they crucified Him and killed Him when He was thirty-three years old. Jesus entered Jerusalem after raising Lazarus from the dead. This is called His triumphal entry; we celebrate this event on Palm Sunday. The city came out and said Hosanna to the King of the Jews. He wanted to present Himself as the Messiah and King of Israel. After His arrest and scourging, the people were disillusioned—they wanted a strong king to overcome the Roman army. They could not accept or believe that their Messiah would come as a Lamb to be sacrificed and not as a Lion to overcome and rule. He came on that day to offer them His kingdom which He would rule when He was age forty but was crucified seven years short. The same Jews who cried, "Hosanna to the king," cried, "Crucify Him." This is what Daniel predicted when he wrote the Messiah would be "cut off" at age thirty-three.

> And after threescore and two weeks shall *Messiah be cut off*, but not for himself: and the people of the prince that shall come shall destroy the city and the sanctuary; and the end thereof shall be with a flood, and unto the end of the war desolations are determined. – Daniel 9:26

At what age was Jesus crucified? Jesus was thirty-three years old. Seven years shy of the two thousand years since the flood. So, it was the year 1,993 years after the flood and 483 years after the Temple dedication. I believe these seven years will be completed after the rapture and during the seven-year tribulation period which is yet to come. After these seven years, we will enter the

Kingdom of God for a thousand years. Here we will live and reign with Jesus our Messiah. This is called the Millennial Kingdom.

After Jesus' death, the world began a period called "The Time of the Gentiles" or the "Time of Grace." It is a time when the church will have dominance in the world. This dispensation or period of time will last two thousand years. This dispensation began when Jesus was thirty-three years old when He ascended into the heavens and promised He would return. This period will end somewhere around the year 2033.

This period of the "Church" began at the Mount of Olives at the ascension of Christ and will end on the Mount of Olives two thousand years later when Christ will return. He ascended at year 33 and will return two thousand years later around the date 2033.

My friends, remember that we are not sure of the exact date of Jesus' birth. We say that it is the year zero but that exact date will never be known. We also know the calendar has had many changes and updates over the last two thousand years. That is why we will never know the exact date, but we can come close. Sometime around the year 2033.

Have you ever wondered why every culture and every tribe or nation follows the same calendar? Why do we all celebrate the same New Year Celebration with crystal balls dropping or fireworks exploding? This same calendar begins at the birth of Jesus Christ. The birth and life of Jesus Christ were so amazing and life-changing that they changed the calendar to emphasize His life and ministry. We have had emperors, we have had dictators, we have had wars, we have had famines, we have had pestilence, we have had plagues, but they have never changed the calendar. One man lived thirty-three years and only ministered for three of those years. He so rocked the world that they changed the calendar. Please say amen.

Oh, there has never been a person like Jesus. After his death and resurrection at age thirty-three years old, he began the church. He was ready to ascend to heaven on the Mount of Olives. He said to his church, go into all the world and preach the Gospel to every creature. In Matthew 24:14, He said to the church that when every creature had heard the Gospel, He would return.

No one is absolutely sure when Jesus will return, but it will be soon! You remember the big ado over the year 2000, called "Y2K." Many said He would return in the year 2000, but they were wrong. It was not from his birth but his ascension that the countdown began. The calendar we use began when Jesus was born—"Merry Christmas." Jesus began this last dispensation or last period at the age of thirty-three.

I remember hearing a Catholic radio station announce they had just got back from the Vatican. "Oh," the announcer said, "They are all amazed and excited." I said to myself, "What are they excited about?" They said the Jubilee is coming. The first Jubilee occurred in 1033 around the time the Orthodox Church and the Catholic Church split. That is, when the Greek Orthodox, the Russian Orthodox Churches split from the Roman Catholic church. Now we are getting ready for another Jubilee where they want to unite the two of them together. That is another prophecy, which I will discuss later.

The year of this second Jubilee is 2033. Now, I do not believe it is going to be exactly 2033 because we really do not have an accurate calendar and have not, because some of the calendars have been changed or altered over these two thousand years. But I want to tell you, it is close. This last period of the church called the "Time of Grace" is coming to a close.

I believe that God set an alarm clock back in Eden during the time of creation and said after a period of seven thousand years just like the seven days of creation it will all come to an end. Now, the Bible says that a day with the Lord is a thousand years and a thousand years as a day. Jesus created the world in six days and on the seventh day, He rested. This period of creation will last seven thousand years. We have labored now for six thousand years. After He returns, we will live and reign with Christ for a thousand years called the Millennial Kingdom. That adds up to seven thousand years.

God does not live in time. You and I live in time. Many of us said, "He or she died," and, "He or she was so young." Age is meaningless to God; it doesn't matter how old we are. What really matters is that you know Jesus as your personal savior. Are you ready?

My wife and I lost our daughter who was seven years old—we were devasted, to say the least. My son, who is a minister today but was only nine years old then, came to me and said, "Dad, I am going to miss Sandy also, but I'm so glad she was saved. Dad, it is time to start believing what you have preached: she is in a better place and is waiting for all of us. Dad, age does not make a difference, she was ready, and God knows best."

What matters to God is whether you have fulfilled your purpose. Are you saved and ready for heaven? The Bible says, "For what shall it profit a man, if he shall gain the whole world, and lose his own soul?" (Mark 8:36). What God is saying is, "Would it profit a man to live 107 years and die without Christ?" Our main purpose in this world is to come to know Christ and then to tell others about our Savior Jesus Christ. The time to accept this "Gift of forgiveness" is now—before all this world comes to an end. Please stop and ask yourself, am I ready to meet God, and am I telling others about my faith in Christ? Do it today!

The first Great Event

I believe we are living in the last days and that the last days began 150 years ago. Remember, 150 years ago, the American Civil War had been fought and industry and technology were increasing. We began to think that we knew it all! Scientists began to teach that there were other theories of how the world came into existence. For most of the past six thousand years, nobody denied there was a creator. They had false gods. They had Jupiter, Zeus, and even Paul preached against the "unknown god." There have been many religions like Islam, Hinduism, Judaism, and Christianity. These all differ in beliefs, but all believe in a greater power who created the world. The Bible states that only a fool would say this all began without a creator. Instead, over the last 150 years, they call us the fools.

Many years ago, while I pastored in Tampa, Florida, I met a man who was a professor at the University of South Florida. He attended a Community Christian Church. He was a deacon. I asked him what he taught at the University of South Florida. He answered geology. Then I asked, "How do you keep your job and remain a creationist?" He answered, "I am not a creationist; I believe in evolution." I responded, "You are a Christian and you believe in evolution?" He said, "Only an ignorant person would not believe in evolution. I have studied the rocks, and the rocks are billions of years old." I said, "I agree that the rocks are billions of years old." He smiled and said, "Oh, are you also an evolutionist?" I said, "No! I believe that God created the world with age. He did not create a baby; He created a man. He did not create an acorn. He created an oak tree. He did not create a seed. He created a plant." He looked shocked. He said, "Oh, I get it now. That makes complete sense! I have never thought of that before."

Now, they have found bones that they said were billions of years old. The only problem is that some of those bones had "cartilage" in them. Do you know what cartilage is? That is the flexible substance in your ears, your nose, and in between the joints in your bones. Cartilage does not last billions of years! Many of those bones are within our timeline of existence. Scientists know this but still call it billions of years old.

We are not being told the truth. They knowingly teach this lie. We have now turned man into an animal. We have taken creation and said that it came about by evolution. We have corrupted our educational system and our children are being corrupted by the teachings, that we are animals and not God's creative children. Your children are being taught lies from the devil and it is no wonder this next generation is falling away from God. How can we teach them that God created the universe?

The Bible proves God created the world

We believe everything was created by God. Look at your wonderful and unbelievable human body. Think about this: a man gets married to his wife, and they can create a child. That's a miracle. You cut your hand and it heals itself. That's a miracle.

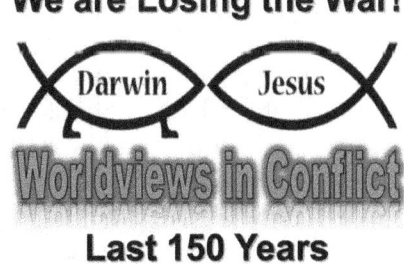

We are losing the battle over the theory of evolution. Many of the churches and many of the pastors today believe in evolution. Most of the Christian colleges teach evolution to a certain extent or totally. In fact, many faculty members cannot keep a job in American colleges if they believe in creation. What are they afraid of?

This evolutionary theory has become a scientific law over the last 150 years and the church has been silent. Have you heard anybody standing up for their rights and beliefs? Have we put our name in and run for the school board? That's the problem in America today. The church has lost its influence.

What do we believe? The Bible says, "In the beginning God created the heaven and the earth" (Genesis 1:1). He created everything we see. In Genesis 1:1–3, two Hebrew words are found in the creation account. The first word is in verse one *bara* ("to create out of nothing"). and then the word *asah* is used in verse three, which means "to make or form." Elohim is the plural word for God and is used because the entire Trinity was involved in the creative event. God the Father made all the substances or matter that we see. Jesus came and took this matter and formed all that we have and then formed man in His own image.

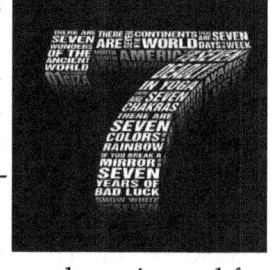

This creative event occurred in six 24-hour days. There are certain teachers who say that each day is an "eon" of time. That's just a compromise to allow for long periods of time. We know each day was a 24-hour period of time because the word *yom* is used for the word "day." The word *yom* means a 24-hour day.

Can I be a scientist for a minute? I was in an anthropology class at the University of North Carolina and the anthropologist said, "You know what's an interesting fact? I've gone on many excavations and excursions where we find new people groups. I do not know why, but all these people have a seven-day week." I said, "That's not funny." Let me share a few more "Funny" facts we see in the world. Why are there seven seas? Why are there seven continents? Why are there seven colors in the rainbow? Ask any musician, Why are there seven tones in the notes? Could it be that God was leaving His fingerprint in this world? And science cannot even figure it out.

Why in the Book of Revelation is the number seven mentioned so often? There is a seven-year tribulation what has seven seals, seven trumpets, and seven bowls of judgment. There are seven churches listed in an order of time from the apostles to our day today. We are living in the last of those churches, the Church of Laodicea.

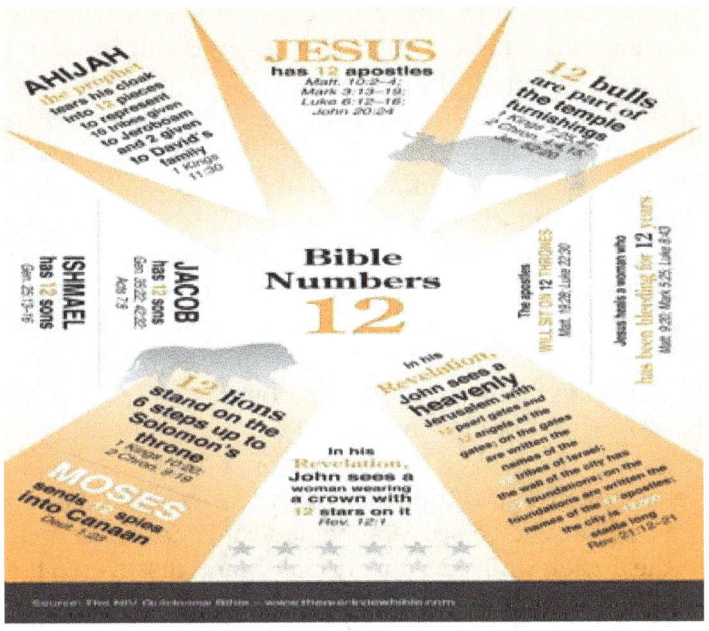

Ask the scientists today, "Why are there 12 months in a year?" I don't know about you, but I'd like to have an extra month. You know why a month is called a "month"?—it comes from the circulation of the moon which is called a "moonth." Ask an evolutionist, Why are there 12 months in a year? Why not 10 or 15? Guess who put that in place.

Why did Jesus choose 12 apostles or why did God choose to have 12 tribes? It was not an accident. My friend, God was putting his fingerprint upon this world and history. "I Am the Creator of all!"

Let me ask any scientist, what is the highest number you can count to? You know what they would say? It is the word infinity. They cannot understand that. Why? It means it just keeps going. There is no end. That's because God wants everybody to know that eternity surrounds you. We live surrounded by Infinity, another fingerprint left by God to show His creative power.

What's the smallest number you can count to? Don't say zero, it is also infinity—negative infinity. Hey, mathematician, can you understand that? You know what they say? I know it is true, but we cannot understand it. They say we just accept it by "faith."

When we build bigger telescopes, there's more of the macro-universe out there. The Hubble telescope expanded our view of our universe. It is bigger than we thought.

It is also true, that when we build stronger microscopes, there's more in the micro-universe. Here are the facts:[1] John Dalton theorizes about the atom in 1808. J. J. Thomson discovers the electron in the 1890s. Ernest Rutherford discovers the nucleus and the proton, the first particle to be discovered in the nucleus of the atom in the 1910s. James Chadwick discovers the neutron, another particle in the nucleus in 1932. Murray Gell-Mann discovered the existence of quarks, the fundamental particles that make up protons and neutrons in 1964. Whichever instrument you use to magnify your view of the universe, it gets Infinitely bigger or smaller. God is leaving another fingerprint saying, "Here I Am!"

Only a fool would not believe in creation. Let's just look at the atom a little deeper. I don't want to give you a science lesson, but let me give you some interesting facts concerning the "Atom." The atom is made of three particles: protons, neutrons, and electrons. The nucleus is where the protons and  neutrons exist. Atoms have the same number of protons as neutrons. Oxygen has eight protons and eight neutrons; carbon has nine. Now, around each nucleus are electrons that move at the speed of light which is 186,000 miles per second. That's how we get electricity. One electron jumps to another, to another, to another. Now, think about this, we talk on a phone over to Italy, they hear us in less than a second. How? our voice moves at 186,000 miles a second.

There is another destructive sign that began also in the last 150 years: the discovery of nuclear power. In our enlightened time, we have invented a way to destroy the entire world: the atomic bomb. 2 Peter 3 tells us that in the last days the elements will burn with a fervor, heat, and fire.

> But the day of the Lord will come as a thief in the night; in the which the heavens shall pass away with a great noise, and the elements shall melt with fervent heat, the earth also and the works that are therein shall be burned up. – 2 Peter 3:10

How did Peter know about "elements"? We only learned of elements and atoms within the last two hundred years. Again, the Bible is ahead of our scientific society. I am reminded of the scripture that says, "What shall it profit a man, if he shall gain the whole world, and lose his own soul?" (Mark 8:36). What shall it profit to gain all this knowledge and allow it to destroy our very world?

Is nuclear power dangerous? We are at a time when North Korea and Iran are on the brink of developing a bomb that could destroy us all. They have both threatened us with nuclear war. What has the United States done? America, under President Obama, gave Iran 150 billion dollars to help them destroy the world. No wonder the doomsday clock is at 11:58. Tick, tick.

Those who are in leadership know the things that I'm telling you are true. They realize how much fear they will spread if they reveal it all. We live like we are on a cruise ship letting the cruise go on and on. All the while, we are being duped every day of our lives. Our foundations are being destroyed.

You see the picture below? It is called the "Doomsday Clock." The clock is set at 11:58, two minutes from doomsday.

I did not make this up. Each year the world leaders look at the world's condition and predict the outlook for the world. It was at 11:55 but they moved it up in January of 2020. They

also see the hot spots in the world like Iran, North Korea, China, and the world Is In a state of unrest. The people that are in the know are telling us to prepare—it will get worse. For we who know Jesus as our Savior and Lord, look up: our redemption draws near.

Evolutionists want you to believe that this evolved. Let me give you another fact that proves creation using the atom. In the nucleus, all the protons have a positive charge. These positive particles should repel each other.

We know that if you take a magnet and put the two positive poles together they repel, but positive and negative charges attract. Why do the protons stay together? What holds the atom together? Uranium has 92 protons in its nucleus. Why do they not repel each other? Why are electrons that have a negative charge not drawn to the protons that have a negative charge?" Ask an evolutionist; their answer: "I don't know." That's because the Bible speaks of Jesus,

> Who is the image of the invisible God, the firstborn of every creature: For by him were all things created, that are in heaven, and that are in earth, visible and invisible, whether they be thrones, or dominions, or principalities, or powers: all things were created by him, and for him: *And he is before all things, and by him all things consist.* – Colossians 1:15–17

Jesus said, "I hold all things together and by me, all things consist." He will hold all things together until the end of the world. How is God going to destroy the world? This is how He's going to do it. Oh, He just lets it go.

How do we know that creation is true? My friends, I liked that children's song: "God said it, and I believe it, and that settles it for me." God said it. We shouldn't even have to go any further, but unfortunately, we must go further. There's more evidence today for creation than there is for evolution.

Have you noticed lately that evolutionists will not debate creationists any longer? Every debate that the creation scientists have with the evolutionist, the creationist has won; not 90 percent, not 98 percent, but 100 percent of the time we win. Each time the evolutionists debate they leave with their tails between their legs. So, guess what they said? "We're not allowing them (Creationists) on campus anymore." And you know what the church said? "Nothing!"

Well as the song says, God said it and I believe it. Where does He say it? Well, let us look at Isaiah 45:18:

> "For thus saith the Lord that created the heavens; God himself that formed the earth and made it; he hath established it, he created it not in vain, he formed it to be inhabited: I am the Lord; and there is none else."

He created it, we should all say, Amen! Now we can just move on. Unfortunately, we cannot, because some of us have been so polluted in our thinking from the schools, PBS, and even Disney with evolutionary lies. Our brains must be retaught, and our children reprogramed with biblical truth. We are losing one generation after another. God help us!

Ask a person today, Where are you going to spend eternity? You know what they say? I hope or I think I am going to heaven. I remember hearing of a professor at Oxford College. He had a young student stand up and said, "Young man, what are your plans?" He said, "Well, I guess I will graduate." "And then what?" He looked around and said, "I guess I will get married. "And then what?" "I guess I will get a good job." The professor said, "And then what?" "I hope I will buy a house and then I would work my job." And again he was asked, "Then what?" "I hope to retire and then I guess I will die." The professor looked sternly at the student and asked, "And then what?" He just shrugged his shoulders and said, "I have no idea." This is where many are today. They have no idea where they came from, why they are here, and where they are going.

This is why creation is so important. If there is no God, there is no creation, if we have no fall from sin, we are not accountable to God, and as a result, there is no eternity and no heaven or hell. Every doctrine in the Bible is important, especially creation.

The universe proves there is a creator God

Why do we believe in creation? Number one, God said it and I believe it. Number two, all of creation proves there is a God. The Bible says so in Romans 1–3, before you get to "all have sinned." God said this: If you look at creation and do not see God, you're a fool and you're without excuse. Psalm 19:1 states, "The heavens declare the glory of God; and the firmament sheweth his handywork." You are not a fool if you look at the world in all its glory and say, "Only God could do this"!

The author of the Book of Job, the oldest book in the Bible, wrote that the earth is suspended in space (Job 26:7). It took us six thousand years to learn that all the universe is suspended in space.

What have others believed? The Egyptians believe the earth was held up by large pillars; the Greeks taught that the god Atlas is holding up the earth. The Hindu belief is the strangest—they believe the earth is held up by a large ele- phant who is standing on two tortoises who are standing on two serpents who are swimming in the eternal sea. Whew! God said it right. In the beginning God created the heavens and the earth.

Let's look at another universal truth: our DNA. Now, think about this: in your body, each cell has 46 chromosomes. When we get married and have children, we pass on 23 chromosomes and our spouse passes on 23 chromosomes for a total of 46. No person ever born has had the same DNA as you have. You are a unique creation of God. Your DNA can be found in every cell in your body: the cells in your nails, your hair, your eyes all of them have the entire story of you. The DNA in every cell of your body has every detail of your entire body. You are able to scratch the inside 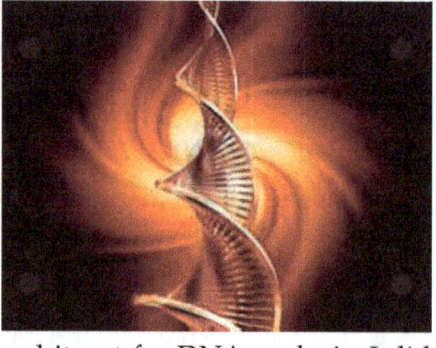 of your mouth and send it out for DNA analysis. I did this and guess what I found out? Number one, I'm alive. Number two, I'm a hundred percent Irish. How did they know that? The whole story of my ancestry was in the cells of my mouth. Wow, that's unbelievable!

Now, think about this for one minute. Are you going to tell me that all this just evolved? If you think this all evolved, then you are a fool.

Let's look at one more of God's great creations: the eyeball. The eyeball is the most unbelievable organ in 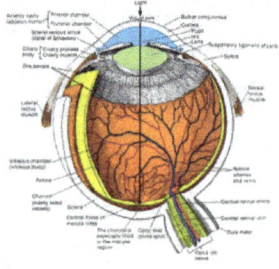 your body. It takes your image, flips it around, and sends it into your brain, the brain flips and interprets the image. My friends, even scientists say this isn't possible. Do you believe this could just evolve, without divine intervention?

Let us look at one more universal proof of creation. We just celebrated the fiftieth anniversary of landing on the moon. Here's what happened. The lunar lander was used to land on the surface of the moon. Look at the legs on the lander: they are 16 feet long. Why 16 feet? Scientists studied the rate of the dust falling to the moon and they said that, since the universe is billions of years old, there would have to be at least 16 feet of dust. So, they made the legs 16 feet long. It was only an inch or so, the amount that would fall over six thousand years.

One-inch imprint in the dust. Could it be true? On July 20, 1969, an estimated 650 million people watched in suspense as Neil Armstrong descended a ladder toward the surface of the Moon. As he took his first steps, he uttered words that would be written into history books. "That's one small step for man. One giant leap for mankind." All of us could see the pictures of that footprint on the moon. It was just an inch deep. You're not going to see that in your textbooks, are you? Why? Because we're being duped. We're being misinformed with known lies and false theories.

Here's what the Bible says in Romans 1:20, "For the invisible things of him from the creation of the world are clearly seen, being understood by the things that are made, even his eternal power and Godhead; so that they are without excuse." Everybody can clearly see the magnitude and greatness of this universe. Someone said if there is a watch (which is very intricately made) there must be a watchmaker. If there is a painting (which only copies God's creation) there must be a painter. When we look at creation, we must conclude there is a creator.

Diversity also proves creation. There has never been another you. Every person who has ever lived is unique. There has never been a snowflake, a grain of sand, or a leaf that is the same. each Is unique and different. God loves diversity. If we all evolved from the same primordial slime, why are we different?

Your conscience proves there is a creator God

Number one, how do we know there's a God? The Bible says there is a God. Number two, how do we know there's a God? The magnitude of the universe proves there is a God. Number three, how do we know there's a God? Your conscience proves there is a God. We all have what some would call a heart-shaped vacuum in our souls that knows there is a God. We can see evidence of this when we see distant tribes believing in idols or false gods.

Even most atheists use the word god before they say a curse. I think it is funny, that those who do not believe in God, are using His name daily. Another funny thing is that I have never heard a man say, "I am an atheist," when he is hanging off the end of the building. They also don't say, "Oh Charles Darwin help me." Guess what they say? "Oh God help me!"

I remember witnessing to a person. I said to him, "You're hanging off a building 17 stories high. Your fingers are starting to give way. What are you going to do?" He said, "Oh, I've thought about that. I would yell out, 'Lord, Jesus save me. Oh, God. Come into my heart. Save me, save me, save me.'" I said, "Why don't you do it today? You may not get a chance to hang off the end of a building." He answered, "No, I will just wait. One day I may."

The Bible says that God put into every man's heart a knowledge of himself and that only a fool would not believe in God. Why are people believing the lie that there is no god? They want to believe that man himself is god. This goes all the way back to the Garden of Eden. God told man not to eat the fruit of good and evil. "For in the day that thou eatest thereof thou shalt surely die" (Genesis 2:17). The devil said, "Ye shall not surely die" (Genesis 3:4). They were "snake bit" and believed the lie and died.

This is still true today. Our young people—and maybe you yourself—watch those scientific shows and are snake bit by Satan's lie. You have been eating the apple. You wanted your eyes to be open and believed his lie, and many will die in their sin and be lost forever.

Evolution has done more to destroy our world than any other of Satan's lies. For the first time in human history, people are denying the creation of God and the very existence of God.

Evolution today

The theory of evolution has also changed history and culture itself. Many of your parents may have fought in World War I or II. My dad fought in World War II. Both of those wars came about because of evolution. Evolution made some evil men think they were the "master race." If evolution is true, they thought they could manipulate genetics to make a master race. And that's exactly what Hitler sought to accomplish.

Many of the leaders of communism developed their atheistic beliefs by following the theory of evolution. The founders of communism, like Stalin, Lenin, Marx, and Engels, were introduced to Darwin and other atheistic thinkers, which brought about their beliefs in communism and a philosophy of atheism. Communism follows the thought that the strong overthrows the weak. This is what Darwin taught. The worst part of evolution is how it changes our philosophy of life and the morals we follow.

The evil leaders of today believe that we can evolve ourselves into a better people. This is called social evolution or social Darwinism. Their answer to improve our society is to eliminate the unnecessary parts of society. How are they doing that? Abortion. Margaret Sanger was a birth control activist and a sex educator. Sanger gave us the term "birth control," and she opened the first

The Beginning of the End

birth control clinic. She also started Planned Parenthood. This organization has killed more than a hundred million babies.

Sanger's worse conclusion from evolutionary thought was the concept of eugenics developed by Francis Galton. Galton believed we could improve our society by increasing people who have good inherited characteristics and disposing of those people who have undesirable characteristics. Historians teach us this is how the Nazi movement began. This is also how the hideous procedure of murder called abortion started. Many adults who Sanger believed

were "feeble-minded" were prevented from having children by forced sterilization. She also showed her racism by supporting the abortion of black children, who she thought were feeble-minded. Today she is held in high esteem for her support of a women's right to abortion.

"The most merciful thing that the large family does to one of its infant members is to kill it."
~ Margaret Sanger
Founder of Planned Parenthood

"I admire Margaret Sanger enormously, her courage, her tenacity, her vision..."
~ Hillary Clinton

How devastating abortion has been to our society and world. Because of evolutionary thinking, we have devalued life. In the United States, we have two states that are allowing babies to be killed after they are born. Oh, God! Help us to see the importance of every

God-created human life. This false evolutionary philosophy also has given us the opposite problem: today we value the life of murders and animals more than a baby's life.

Sadly, the church is silent. Many people who call themselves Christian are voting for pro-abortion candidates. They must be ignorant or seriously brainwashed for allowing this murder to continue. If somebody says, I'm "pro-life," does that make the other person "pro-death"? They would like to think they are "pro-choice," but in reality, they are "pro-death." If you are "pro-choice," why are you not giving that baby a choice? Sanger began Planned Parenthood because she wanted to wipe out the black race, which she felt was inferior to other races.

Yes! Evolutionary thought started two wars, the idea of abortion, and racism. How has evolution brought an increase in racism? We started looking at other people as inferior to ourselves. We began to believe that only the strongest and smartest should survive.

Conclusion

The first Great Event that I believe will bring about the second coming of Christ is the belief that there is no God and that we evolved without divine intervention. All five Great Events began in the last 150 years. One hundred and fifty years ago, the devil brought this theory of evolution into our society, and now it has become the rule and the basis of our society. The world we live in has become indoctrinated to the false teaching and the philosophy of evolution. We have been "snake bit" and you don't even know it.

My friends, it is time to take a stand for what we believe. We have been on the slippery slope since the time we were born. The devil had manipulated us through our schools, governments, and media. Even many of our churches have been deceived. Unfortunately, many churches today deny the deity of Christ and the accuracy and inspiration of the Bible.

Is Jesus coming again? Yes! And He said He will return when the world is like the days of Noah. I believe we have been living in the days of Noah for the past 150 years. What are the signs that have appeared in the last 150 years, that show we are living in the days of Noah? We will be discussing them each in detail in this book.

There has been another movement started over the last 150 years called "Globalism." Many people call it the Illuminati, or the "New World Order." The Bushes, the Clintons, and the Obamas were all "Globalists." Do you know the Clintons and the Bushes are best friends? Do you know that Bill Clinton was called the fourth Bush brother? President Trump is the first president elected since Ronald Reagan, who has not been a Globalist. That means they do not believe in a One World government.

The Globalist theme is "Let's bring the whole world together." The thought of world unity sounds great but without God and Jesus Christ as the unifiers, there can be no peace or unity. History has proven that. The Bible predicts a "One World government." It will appear in the last days and the antichrist will rule with an iron fist.

Another sinful event that has erupted in the last 150 years is the destruction of families and marriage. For six thousand years, babies were born into families of a mother and father, and not born out of wedlock. Well, they were some, but it was not acceptable. For the first time in human history, more babies are born out of wedlock than into a home with a mother and father. History has shown that many people had five or six wives, but they still got married before they had children. You know why? Because they believed God created their babies and they were special. Today, two men or two women can adopt children, and this is considered acceptable.

Another event that has occurred in the last 150 years is the increase in speed, education, worldwide travel, and communication. Many of these inventions bring about pollution and disease. Today our population is eight billion, and our world is so filthy and so corrupt that even if God does not destroy the world it will destroy itself. All these things were predicted as happening before the second coming of Jesus Christ.

Another sinful event that will precede the second coming is a "falling away from the church." Why are people falling away from the church? Because the churches are falling away from the truth of God's Word. Jesus predicted that the church would lose its doctrinal stance.

We have Pope Francis in the Roman Catholic Church who is an evolutionist and a socialist. He has recently said, "God is not a…magician. … Evolution in nature is not inconsistent with the notion of creation, because evolution requires the creation of beings that evolve."[2] He has been quoted as saying that Muslims go to heaven, atheists go to heaven, everybody goes to heaven. Isn't that wonderful? He is a liar and he has been placed there by Satan.

Friends, it's time for the church to be the church. We need to be "intolerant." There's nothing in the Scripture to tell us to be tolerant. It is time for us to get angry. Our world is being taken away and we need to stand up and say we believe the Word of God! We need to change this culture. That is what revival is about. "If my people, which are called by my name, shall humble themselves, and pray, and seek my face, and turn from their wicked ways; then will I hear from heaven, and will forgive their sin, and will heal their land" (2 Chronicles 7:14). God is demanding we take a stand. Many today say, "I do not want to get involved." That is the problem. We, the church, are the only hope for America and the world!

SECOND GREAT EVENT

The Flood – Violence and Immorality

This book is about the beginning and the end. I believe that the first 12 chapters of Genesis give us clues to the end of the world. I believe we are living in the last days before the return of Jesus Christ. We believe that Jesus was born (Merry Christmas), died on the cross (Good Friday), and rose from the dead (Happy Easter). This is what we call the "Gospel Story." But here is more! Jesus is coming again! I believe we can see evidence of the fact, that Jesus is coming very soon! We are indeed living in the last days.

I believe these last days began 150 years ago. Many prophetic writers and preachers look on much of the last thirty years or forty years as the last days. Yes! It is certainly getting worse, but the last hundred and fifty years is a time we have never seen before.

It all started with the Industrial Revolution, the telephone, the television, movies, cars, planes, rocket ships, and satellites. All of this came about in the last 150 years. It was all predicted as being a part of the last days. Daniel 12:4 says, "But thou, O Daniel, shut up the words, and seal the book, even to the time of the end: many shall run to and fro, and knowledge shall be increased." These prophetic "events" have been recorded in recent history. We have never seen these many unbelievable and ultra-scientific technologies. The discovery of atomic power and the increase of knowledge was predicted by the Prophet Daniel.

Here is where we begin. Only in these last 150 years have we started denying the creation of the world and the existence of God. I am sad to say, evolution and atheism are now the accepted philosophy and are accepted as scientific fact today.

Last 150 Years
- Beginning Denying of God
- Conflict between Jews & Arabs
- Beginning New World Order
- Destruction of the "Family"
- Discovery of Atomic Power
- Increase Speed & Knowledge
- Worldwide Travel & Communication - TV

There is not one fact that supports or proves evolution. Have you seen a missing link? I have seen some people that look like they were a missing link. There are none! You cannot reproduce outside your species. The Bible says God created each species to reproduce after their "kind"—the word "kind" is the biblical word for species. You cannot mate or exchange genes outside your own species. There is no multiplication without a genetic connection. It has never been done. It can't be done in the laboratory. It's just impossible.

We are living in a time today where scientists are trying to manipulate God's creation. How? Cloning, the changing or manipulating of DNA. My friends, we must be careful of this. This is God's creation. There are godly rules to follow. When we mess with God's perfect creation and add or change it, we negatively mutate and destroy whatever we are trying to improve. It is *never* an improvement. We have not only delved into DNA and species manipulation but have opened Pandora's box by releasing atomic power by breaking apart the atom, God's building block.

I remember when I was a boy, probably about 11 years old, and we went to New York City. We were in this building, about the size of a football stadium.

All the sixth graders are all around the side on a raised platform. And suddenly, we heard this noise. There was a huge instrument in the middle of the arena, probably the size of a semi-truck. It had a big globe on it, like a satellite. Then we heard a loud roaring sound, becoming louder and louder! This deafening sound inside the arena was now as loud as a jet engine. And then suddenly, several bolts of lightning shot out from this instrument, lighting up the entire arena.

I later found out what they did: they split the atom. I probably was radiated but they didn't know anything about radiation back then. I probably walked out of the arena glowing that day. It was lucky it was not night, as we would have lit up the streets.

That small atom held eternal, unbelievable power. We did not realize what we were unleashing. Only in these last days has science unleashed this supernatural atomic power. We now live with the threat of nuclear war.

Many of today's new technological inventions have terrible repercussions and create life-threatening pollution. But it can be worse: the splitting of the atom is going to bring about the destruction of the world. Read with me in the /where it speaks of the last days. We read in 2 Peter 3:10, "But the day of the Lord will come as a thief in the night; in the which the heavens shall pass away with a great noise, and the elements shall melt with fervent heat, the earth also and the works that are therein shall be burned up."

The world will burn with the "elements" and it will melt. What does the word element mean? Elements are the same as atoms. Everything in the world is made of "Elements" or "Atoms."

We are moving toward a worldwide nuclear proliferation of atomic bombs. We now have the power to destroy the entire world. God help us! This power is now in the hands of many of the world's most dangerous countries. North Korea and Iran are just two of the many countries.

I believe this "melting of the elements" will bring about the tribulation period. You remember how our world stopped because of September 11; on that day only three thousand died. A single atomic bomb could kill millions. An atomic blast bomb could melt the ice caps. If those ice caps melt, most of the world would feel the devastation.

The Bible says in Revelation 16:20, "And every island fled away, and the mountains were not found." The islands will disappear; the coastlines will disappear.

This nuclear devastation and the repercussions that will follow will so devastate this world that whoever the leader is (antichrist) he will enact martial law and force the world to be numbered and classified. He wants to know who is a follower of his domain. He will force all the inhabitants of the earth to put a mark upon their hands or their foreheads. This mark will be 666 or a designation of 6+6+6. The Bible says that no man will be able to buy or sell without the Mark of the Beast.

It will not come about voluntarily. It will occur because some kind of cataclysmic event will force all who need food and supplies to take the "Mark of the Beast." Why is this going to occur? Because we are manipulating God's creation, which can and will destroy ourselves.

Another issue we see on the nightly news is the discussions about "The New World Order" or "Globalism." Friends, we in the United States have two main parties today. Both parties have many who believe in globalism.

They do not believe in a separate United States. They want the United States to be a part of a United World, and part of the New World Order. Donald Trump tried to change the politics of Globalism by putting America first. The powers of the world and America turned against him. Brexit is another block that has held back this globalism. The future of politics will revolve around Globalism and global warming.

It will not last long. We are drifting to become like Europe. The European Common Market has successfully united Europe into one unified "Union of Countries" This is part of the antichrist's plan.

Review

Let us look at God's timeline of His creation. From the time of creation to the time of the flood, two thousand years, from the time of the flood to the time of Christ, how long? 1,993 years.

This event brings us to the Book of Daniel. Daniel was written in the time when Israel was in captivity, guess where they were? They were in Iraq and Iran. Isn't it funny that now we're talking about Iraq and Iran?

> Know therefore and understand, that from the going forth of the commandment *to restore and to build Jerusalem unto the Messiah the Prince* shall be seven weeks, and threescore and two weeks: the street shall be built again, and the wall, even in troublous times. And after threescore and two weeks shall *Messiah be cut off*, but not for himself: and the people of the prince that shall come shall destroy the city and the sanctuary; and the end thereof shall be with a flood, and unto the end of the war desolations are determined. And he shall confirm the *covenant with many for one week*: and in the midst of the week he shall cause the

sacrifice and the oblation to cease, and for the overspreading of abominations he shall make it desolate, even until the consummation, and that determined shall be poured upon the desolate. – Daniel 9:25–27

This prophecy was written five hundred years before Christ was born. Daniel prophesied that the Temple was going to be rebuilt, and from the time of the Temple to the birth of the Messiah was 490 years. Then the Messiah will establish His kingdom and be crowned King of Kings.

That is why the wise men, who came from Babylon (Iraq and Iran), came to Bethlehem and presented Him gifts fit for a king. They came from a group of Magi who were followers of the Prophet Daniel. This group of Magi studied the Scriptures and knew the Messiah was to come in 490 years.

They also studied the stars and saw a strange starlight, forty years before the predicted 490 years that Daniel predicted Messiah would come to rule. This is the Messiah's star. So, they traveled from Iraq and Iran (Babylon) to Bethlehem and presented gifts to Jesus as the predicted King.

As the gospels tell us, Jesus was crucified at thirty-three years of age ("cut off" as Daniel predicted) and the calendar stopped at 483 years, seven years short of the predicted 490 years. After Jesus' resurrection, Jesus gathered his disciples together and began a new dispensation or period of time called the "Church" or the time of "Grace." This dispensation of the church would also span two thousand years.

After two thousand years, Jesus would return and take His church home (the rapture). After the rapture, God will send seven years of tribulation. The world has never seen such plagues and problems. At the end of this seven-year tribulation period, Jesus will return and enter Jerusalem again, as He did at the triumphal entry. This time He will return as "King of Kings and Lord of Lords."

The Bible states that at the end of this dispensation of the church there will be a "great falling away."

> Now we beseech you, brethren, by the coming of our Lord Jesus Christ, and by our gathering together unto him, That ye be not soon shaken in mind, or be troubled, neither by spirit, nor by word, nor by letter as from us, as that the day of Christ is at hand. Let no man deceive you by any means: for that day shall not come, except there come a falling away first, and that man of sin be revealed, the son of perdition. – 2 Thessalonians 2:1–3

Five hundred years ago the reformation of the church began, sending a great outpouring of the Holy Spirit. Many mainline Protestant denominations began, and the Gospel spread around the world.

Unfortunately, most of these denominations have slid into apostasy and liberalism. These many denominations deny the truth of God's Word and have accepted the wisdom of this world.

The Bible says in the "Last Days" we will be called the church of Laodicea, "The Lazy (Lukewarm) Church." Revelation 3:14–17 says,

> "And unto the angel of the church of the Laodiceans write; These things saith the Amen, the faithful and true witness, the beginning of the creation of God; I know thy works, that thou art neither cold nor hot: I would thou wert cold or hot. So then because thou art lukewarm, and neither cold nor hot, I will spue thee out of my mouth. Because thou sayest, I am rich, and increased with

goods, and have need of nothing; and knowest not that thou art wretched, and miserable, and poor, and blind, and naked."

Today these so-called churches deny the Virgin birth, the deity of Christ, and the inspiration of the Word of God. They even deny the very existence of God. God help us!

We are living in that day. Most of the churches, some say over 70 percent of the churches, are dying or are in a steady rate of decline. We are seeing the death of God's living church. Of the 30 percent of believing churches, they are only hearers of Word but are not doers of the Word.

When did Jesus begin this "Church dispensation"? He started the church when He was thirty-three years old. The calendar year was 33. It is predicted to end around the year 2033, or around that time. I am not giving a date. This calendar we use today has been changed, altered, and revamped many times over these past two millennia. I may not know the exact date but, it is going to be soon!

Jesus is going to come back to call us home (this is called the rapture of the church) and then comes the last seven years of judgment called the great tribulation.

> For then shall be *great tribulation*, such as was not since the beginning of the world to this time, no, nor ever shall be. – Matthew 24:21
>
> And at that time shall Michael stand up, the great prince which standeth for the children of thy people: and there shall be a *time of trouble*, such as never was since there was a nation even to that same time: and at that time thy people shall be delivered, every one that shall be found written in the book. – Daniel 12:1
>
> Immediately after the *tribulation* of those days shall the sun be darkened, and the moon shall

not give her light, and the stars shall fall from heaven, and the powers of the heavens shall be shaken. – Matthew 24:29

And I said unto him, Sir, thou knowest. And he said to me, These are they which came out of *great tribulation*, and have washed their robes, and made them white in the blood of the Lamb. – Revelation 7:14

After the seven years of tribulation and Jesus fulfills all His prophecies, He will be coronated as King of Kings and Lord of Lords. We (the saved) will live and reign with Jesus for a thousand years.

Remember what I wrote in the first chapter: two thousand years from creation to the flood, two thousand years from the flood to the Time of Christ, and two thousand years from Christ's ascension to His second coming. This is just like creation's seven days: six days God created and on the seventh, He rested. Remember, God said in 2 Peter 3:8: "But, beloved, be not ignorant of this one thing, that one day is with the Lord as a thousand years, and a thousand years as one day." He was showing us in creation how long this created world would last.

God tells us to be prepared. His creation is like an alarm clock and the alarm clock is set to go off in the seven thousandth year. Only God the Father knows this time and date. He will destroy all of His creation by His word and then "re-create" all of creation and make it all new, and then the saved will live with God for eternity. Have you made your preparations?

God has left His fingerprint in His creation, so that man could see His influence and know there is a God in heaven. Every tree, snowflake, star, grain of sand, and every person are completely different. Each one of these is distinct and different. Think about that! None of them is the same. God loves diversity. If they evolve from the same place and same essence, would they not all be the same? I think of all the people that have ever been born—not one has had my fingerprint, not one has had my DNA. "We are fearfully and wonderfully made." Evolution cannot answer the question: Where do kindness, love, and compassion come from? These are attributes of God that God has given to His creation.

Why is this diversity so important? God made you unique and loves you just as you are. He knows all about your weaknesses and sins and loves you unconditionally. He has a wonderful plan for your life. Please call out to God as I did and become a follower of Jesus Christ.

When will all this conclude and the end of the world? We are now at the beginning of the end and I believe the first 12 chapters of Scripture tell us when the second coming of Christ will occur. Our key passage is found in 2 Peter 3:1–4,

> This second epistle, beloved, I now write unto you; in both which I stir up your pure minds by way of remembrance: That ye may be mindful of the words which were spoken before by the holy prophets, and of the commandment of us the apostles of the Lord and Savior: *Knowing this first, that there shall come in the last days scoffers*, walking after their own lusts, And saying, Where is the promise of his coming? for since the fathers fell asleep, all things continue as they were *from the beginning of the creation*.

When we look at the beginning of creation, we are going to see what will happen before the end of the world.

The second Great Event

There are five major events in the first 12 chapters that point to the second coming of Christ. Number one is creation. For the first time in human history, we've denied the creation of the world. Secondly, the flood. Jesus said, As the days of Noah were, so shall it be in the last days.

Let us begin in the time of Noah. What does God's Word say?

> And, behold, I, even I, do bring a *flood of waters* upon the earth, to destroy all flesh, wherein is the breath of life, from under heaven; and every thing that is in the earth shall die. – Genesis 6:17
>
> And spared not the old world, but saved Noah the eighth person, a preacher of righteousness, bringing in the *flood upon the world* of the ungodly. – 2 Peter 2:5
>
> And as it was in the *days of Noe*, so shall it be *also in the days of the Son of man*. They did eat, they drank, they married wives, they were given in marriage, until the day that Noah entered into the ark, and the *flood came*, and destroyed them all. – Luke 17:26–27
>
> Which sometime were disobedient, when once the longsuffering of God waited in the *days of Noah*, while the ark was a preparing, wherein few, that is, eight souls were saved by water. – 1 Peter 3:20

Now, what happened at this time? First, nations began; second, the races began; also, the seasons began. They never had a fall or winter before the flood. Here atheism began and the mocking of God's preacher.

The world was polluted and filled with violence. Sexual diseases were killing the people. Just like Sodom. God had to destroy the world, or the world would have destroyed itself.

Can I tell our young people about sexual diseases? Children today, before they go to school, must have

 injections for venereal diseases. It is mandatory. They are telling us that 60 to 70 percent of our young people are already infected with some kind of venereal disease. We are living in a filthy, sick, and perverted world, just as it was in the days before the flood.

Let us look at one of these diseases, AIDS. AIDS came to us from the apes who are able to live with the AIDS virus without dying. Man had sexual relations (bestiality) with an ape and contracted AIDS and have passed on this filthiness to the world.

In all of these six thousand years, nobody ever thought of cohabitating with an animal until the last days, and these diseases are rampant in some communities. Another source of disease comes from the homosexual community. These sexual diseases come because the homosexual community is using the "plumbing" that God had created for our reproduction in the wrong way. These diseases are destroying the world like in the days of Noah.

Why were Noah and his family chosen? They had not contracted these diseases from the world. Their bloodlines were pure. Genesis 6:8–9 says, "But Noah found *grace* in the eyes of the Lord. These are the generations of Noah: Noah was a *just man* [not contaminated] and *perfect* in his generations, and Noah walked with God." He did not walk with wicked men.

Let us look at this pre-flood world. The world used to be perpendicular, straight up. It was covered with a thick water vapor (Firmament) which caused a greenhouse effect. No matter where you went in the world, you could be in the Antarctic and it was perfect weather. It had a perfect greenhouse environment. Everywhere you went, it was perfect. Things grew large and people lived to be hundreds of years old. All the vegetation was full of nourishment. There were no harmful effects of the sun. It was beautiful. Everything was rich and full of life. But, in a mere two thousand years mankind had destroyed it.

> And God saw that the *wickedness of man was great* in the earth, and that every imagination of the thoughts of his heart was only *evil continually*. And it *repented the Lord* that he had made man on the earth, and it grieved him at his heart. And the Lord said, *I will destroy* man whom I have created from the face of the earth; both man, and beast, and the creeping thing, and the fowls of the air; for it repenteth me that I have made them. – Genesis 6:5–7

I believe God came and tilted the earth. He tilted it at a perfect 23.5-degree angle. If God had made it 24 degrees we would all be dead; 22 degrees, we would all be dead. But 23.5 degrees kept us a perfect slant to allow for seasons. It was a perfect distance from the sun and the perfect slant allowed half of our planet to be either closer or further away from the sun, thus causing the seasons.

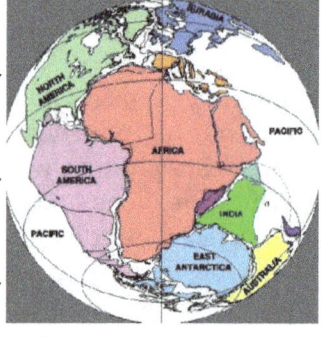

Many ask, "What happened to all the water?" Because of this perfect tilt, much of the water froze and formed the two polar caps. By tilting the earth, it causes the ends of our planet to be farther away from the sun and be extremely cold. The rest of the water formed the seven seas and the thousands of worldwide lakes. We have found animals frozen in this ice. This would be impossible if it took billions of years to freeze. The animal would have decayed. Instead, we find these animals perfectly frozen.

The Bible describes the flood

Why do we believe in the biblical flood? Number one, the Bible declared it and Jesus described it. Jesus says to us in Matthew 24, As the days of Noah, so shall it be in the last days. How was it the time of Noah? They were marrying and giving in marriage. They were killing their unborn or newborn. They would sacrifice their young to false gods. They would throw their young on a large heated pan. These pans would be 10 feet wide, and underneath they would light a fire. They would throw their babies onto the pan and watch their babies fry.

It is worse today! Today, we are going inside the womb of a woman and ripping the child apart, burning its skin, tearing it apart, or allowing the head to come out and cutting its throat. Today cities and states are allowing babies to be born only to watch them die, then let them lie there crying until they are dead. Unfortunately, the church is silent.

Many pastors today say, We don't want to get involved in politics. That is exactly what was happening during the time of Noah. But not Noah—he got involved in politics. Noah took a stand and went against the majority. He stood for God and His Word. He continued to preach and warn of the coming judgment.

We must remember that this boat was built on dry ground. Can you imagine? They had never even seen it rain. "What is rain?" Yet Noah continued to preach, "Folks, it is going to rain." They said, "Noah you are a fool!" Yet he continued preaching for over 120 years! Today, conservative, Bible-believing preachers are called fools. These believers are telling all of us it is going to get worse. Sadly, many preachers are falling by the wayside, left and right, but the ones that are not are being called foolish. May we all stay "foolish" until Jesus returns.

Let us turn to Genesis 6:8, one of my favorite verses: "But Noah found grace in the eyes of the Lord." The Bible says he was "perfect." Do you know what perfect means? It meant he was not infected by the world's disease or it's sinful influence. He and his children were not infected with the diseases that were around them.

It didn't mean that he was perfect: we are all sinners. We are saved by the grace of God. God looked all over the world and tried to find somebody who lived a life of purity. God found it in Noah and his family. If God had not destroyed the world, those diseases would have eventually killed everybody. Again, Noah and his family are the only eight people who had not been infected by the diseases.

And God said, "I am going to give all of you grace. Please, stay pure for three hundred years, continue to preach and be an example to the world as you build the Ark." Noah followed and walked with God. He would not bend, and he stood on God's Word and was not contaminated by the world.

Flood stories around the world

Why must we believe in a real flood? First, God's word declared it and Jesus describes it. Second, every culture in our world has a variety of stories about a flood and a man who was a captain who saves all the people. In the last 150 years, we have found hundreds of people groups that had never seen civilized people. Do you know that 59 of them had a story about Noah? Do you know that in the Chinese and Viking histories there is a story about Noah? Why do we not as a culture believe in Noah? Society today calls it a fairy tale. It is no fairy tale!

There is worldwide evidence of the flood. Number one, there have been many sightings from people who said they have seen the remains of the Ark on the top of Mount Ararat, in Turkey. Secondly, the Grand Canyon is a living laboratory that proves the fact of a worldwide flood. When I was studying the Grand Canyon in geology class, the professor told us it took billions and billions of years for a little trickling of water to form the Grand Canyon. Yes, if it were a trickling of water, but it could take a short time with tens of millions of gallons of water going through year after year. Recently, creation scientists were not allowed in the canyon because they found absolute evidence for the flood. They found evidence that evolution was false by the pattern of the layers in the Grand Canyon. The creationist showed an upward sweep on the strata in the rock layer. If the water slowly eroded the rock, the strata would show a downward sweep.

But these lines went up. If it deteriorated slowly, the lines would go down. This evidence found that it was a lot of water in a relatively short time which caused this erosion. When the Trump Administration came in, the creationist was once again given entrance. What is the evolutionist afraid of?

Another fact that proves there was a worldwide flood is how the pyramids and sphinx show they were covered with water. There is also evidence of erosion, especially on the face of the sphinx, which could only be explained by massive amounts of water.

How were the seven seas formed and why are there seven seas? The seven seas came from the eroded water that covered the land. After the flood ended, all the water drained off the land to form the seven seas. Like a plow breaking up the land, this massive amount of water

The Beginning of the End

Marine Sediments and Fossils On Mt Everest

"The Qomolangma Formation, the highest section of rock on the summit pyramid of Mount Everest, is made of layers of Ordovician-age limestone, recrystallized dolomite, siltstone, and laminae...The **upper layers have many marine fossils**, including **trilobites**, **crinoids**, and **ostracods**..." (a layer) "at the bottom of the summit pyramid contains the remains of microorganisms, including cyanobacteria deposited in shallow warm water." From: www.thoughtco.com/geology-of-mount-everest-755308 Similar info from en.wikipedia.org/wiki/Mount_Everest

Nautiloid from Tibhes Region of Himalayas 17,000' JSL pix

ripped through the seven continents around the world. We see evidence of this throughout the world. There are seven platonic plates that make up the seven continents. These plates were and are constantly moving.

Look at this fossil it was found on the top of Mount Everest. Now, let me ask you a question, how did that fish fossil get up there? Guess how the evolutionists answer this question? "We don't know!" The creationist has the answers. Could it be that Noah's Ark and the flood is true? Of course, it is true.

Let us look at the seven continents of the world. The earth is about 71 percent water and 29 percent land. The seven continents of the world, which make up this 29 percent, were once joined together as a single massive landmass. But due to plate tectonics, they gradually broke apart and separated. All the water eroded from the land to form the seven seas. The earth is like a big puzzle that all fits together. That's why Europe, North America, Africa, South America, Antarctica, and the Arctic all fit together perfectly.

Why do we keep hearing the number seven? God has left His fingerprint in His creation. The number seven is found everywhere. There are seven notes in a scale of music, seven colors of the rainbow. The number seven is the perfect number on the PH scale of water. If the PH is higher, it is acidic; if the PH is lower, it is a base. There are also seven seas and seven continents. The number seven is seen everywhere in this world and our history. Why? God reminds us, "Wherever you go, whatever arts you follow in music or sciences, you're going to see My name." Yet they still deny it.

This is why God told the people of the world at the Tower of Babel to spread out and multiply. God knew the world's continents were about to spread out. They refused and God forced them by confusing their speech. It worked.

Each of the landmasses (plates) started separating along fault lines. They are still moving today. If the plates stop moving, an earthquake will occur. The Bible says in the "Last Days" there will be an increase in earthquakes, just like after the flood. This is happening just as it was written. Scientists call our time today the "Age of Earthquakes."

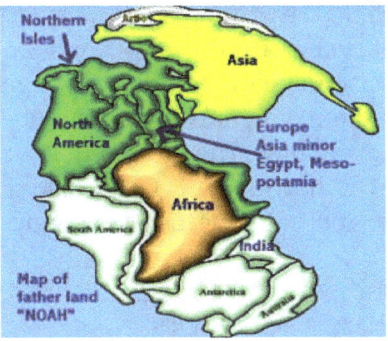

As the plates moved and the water filled the chasms, the seven seas were formed. As the water receded to form the oceans all the minerals of the land leeched into the oceans. Therefore all oceans are full of minerals and salts.

The world, when created, was covered by a blanket of moisture. It caused a greenhouse effect, with perfect weather, like the rainforests today. This caused everything to grow huge. Why is this so important? This is where all the water came from. Also, God lifted the earth and water came out from the ground like gushers of water. We can see the destruction water can bring with hurricanes and floods. It takes months to repair from them.

This happened worldwide: water gushing out and then the firmament falling down in rain. It rained for forty days and forty nights and covered over all the landmasses. Then God, in His miraculous hand, moved the

tectonic plates, forming the continents, mountains, and canyons. During the time of Noah, there was a tremendous increase in earthquakes. Everywhere they went, the ground shook because God was shaking the world.

We have seen the number of earthquakes increase in modern days. They do not even make the news anymore. When I was a kid, one earthquake made the front page. Now there are so many of them, you only hear about the most devastating large earthquakes. The ground that we are living on is moving even now. Why is God shaking the world again? Because God is telling us to wake up! "I'm coming again."

One race, three ancestors

Creation teaches us that we all come from one race. No one in this world should hold a bias or prejudice against another race. Now, my anthropology class taught us we all descended from three different people groups. Scientists today have learned that all people are descended from three genetically unique mothers. This is exactly what the Bible teaches. Noah's three daughters-in-law give us the three needed different unique DNA traits. The Bible is correct again!

I am of Irish descent, and most people describe me as a very white man. They are 100 percent wrong. No one is all white or all black. We are all "colored." Adam, Eve, and Noah were all dark-skinned. We can genetically lose pigment, but it is different to gain pigment. All of us are a shade of some color. Some of us have a darker shade of skin, some of us are a lighter shade of skin.

We are all one race. Every one of us is part of a dying race. We are all a sinful race. We all need the same Savior. God wants all of us to go to the same destination, heaven. There is only one way to heaven, through Jesus.

All the world descended from three different nations: Asians, Africans, and Europeans. Each of them represents one of the three sons of Noah.

The three sons of Noah gave us three cultures and three great nation groups. In the Bible, the number three is very important. When the wise men came to Jesus they brought three gifts, one to represent each of the three sons of Noah. On the day of Pentecost in Acts 2, Peter preached to the Asians, to the Europeans, and to the Africans. Three people groups. Then we look in the Book of Revelation concerning the last days. The Bible says the antichrist will bring in three kings, the king of the South from Africa, the king of the East from Asia, and the king of the North from Europe.

When will these three kingdoms join together? In the last days, the antichrist will lead three kingdoms North, South, and East, to invade Israel. The Bible is putting everything together and telling us today to listen, to wake up, and to get ready.

Hannibal, who tried to use elephants to go over the Himalayas mountains, failed because it was too high and too cold. The kingdom from the East could not enter Israel for millennia, but today it is possible. A highway was completed in 1979, called the Karakoram Highway, formally known as the China-Pakistan Friendship Highway. It is a 1,300 km road that links Pakistan to China.

Why is this important? The Book of Revelation says that the Kingdom of the East will invade Israel. "And the number of the army of the horsemen were two hundred thousand thousand" (Revelation 9:16). Recently, China counted their army: 3.9 million. China's population in 2018 was 1.393 billion. The Kingdom of the East can now come across the Himalayans due to the Karakoram Highway.

The second kingdom, the king of the North, is said to come down into Israel. Ezekiel 37–38 tells us who this kingdom may be. Russia and the European Union is this third kingdom. There was a time when we were making friends with Russia, but now all we hear about is the Russian collusion. It's all part of the plan. Every country in the European Union is against the State of Israel.

The third, the Kingdom of the South, is described, and nations are listed. The Bible lists 11 nations that are coming from the South and they are the exact same nations of the Muslim brotherhood. Most of these nations have had their dictator leaders deposed in the last 10 years.[3]

Today, Iran's radical Islamist alliance is forming around Iraq, Libya, Lebanon, Yemen, Ethiopia, Egypt, and part of Sudan. While some of this territory lies east of the Holy Land, most of it is located to the south. The Bible calls this power the king of the south, and Iran already strongly influences or is allied with these nations south of Israel.

All three of these Kingdoms will come together in a place called Megiddo—this is the valley where the final battle called Armageddon will be fought. "And he gathered them together into a place called in the Hebrew tongue Armageddon" (Revelation 16:16). This land area (Megiddo) is in the northern part of Israel and connects Israel to the entire world. Many world battles have been fought in Megiddo.

This area is surrounded by several mountains where great miracles have been done. One was where Jesus appeared with the Godhead on the Mount of Transfiguration. Another is where Deborah held back the Philistines from coming into Israel. On one side is where Elijah called down fire from heaven. This valley is a historic place, but in the future, this is where the world will come to an end. In the near future, the king of the East, the king of the North, and the king of the South will all join together with the antichrist, at Armageddon to do battle against God.

The world in its foolishness thinks that bombs, cannons, and nuclear power can destroy the Son of God. Jesus will come as King of Kings and Lord of Lords; He will come with His now-glorified church. How will God destroy the world? God, who created the world with His spoken Word, will destroy the world the same way. The spoken Word of God will come forth and destroy it completely.

Conclusion

We have looked at the flood historically, now we will look at it prophetically. Noah had three sons.

Shem, the eldest son of Noah, had five sons. Shem was the father of the Jewish and Arab people, known as the Semitic nations. Shem is always mentioned first and most believe he was the oldest. He was also blessed by his descendants; they were called to be the chosen people of God.

Ham, is the middle of Noah's three sons. Ham himself had four sons, Cush (Ethiopia), Mizraim (Egypt), Put (Libya), and Canaan (Canaanite). The Bible states that Ham and his sons lived and became the forefathers of the African continent.

Japheth, the youngest son of Noah, had seven sons who became the forefathers of the European people.

The Bible says that in the last days perilous times will come. Just as the days of Noah. How was it?

People lived in great fear because there was violence everywhere. I grew up outside New York City, in a town off the coast of Long Island. It was a tough area but, we never locked our doors. In fact, we never even owned a key to our home. Nobody ever broke into our home. But now, you can have six locks and a security system and still be robbed.

Why? Because we are living in the days of Noah. Today, women are afraid to walk outside alone, but there was a time if you saw a lady or a man walking down the street, you would pull over and give her or him a ride in your car.

Thirty years ago, we used to let our kids go out and play; not so today. Today, we cannot let our kids go out and play because we are afraid that a pedophile or pervert will pick them up and abuse them. We are living in a sick and perverted world.

It is time to wake up. The church is asleep while the world destroys itself and is becoming more and more sinful. Why is the church sleeping? Christians have seen so much sin that we have become used to it, and nothing shocks us anymore. In our world today, right is wrong, and wrong is right. Oh God, give us a revival!

How was it in the days of Noah? There was a population explosion. It is called the "exponential curve." Let me illustrate. If I gave you a penny every day and doubled it every day, how much money do you have in one month? 10.7 million dollars. What do you have on the thirty-first day? 21.4 million. What do you have on the thirty-third day? What do you have on the thirty-fifth day? This is what anthropologists called a J-shaped curve.

We are living in a J-shaped population curve today. We are trying to end it, or at the least try to slow down this deadly curve. This is why abortion is popular, and why we started the space program.

We are all living on one big spaceship, the spaceship planet earth. We are traveling at 67,000 miles per hour. There is only so much water, which will be what the next war will be fought over, especially in the Middle East.

There is only so much food, which can become worse with weather and worldwide disasters. In Africa today, locusts are devastating crops. This problem becomes worse when some people have too much food and some have very little or no food. The Bible says that in the last days it will cost a day's labor to buy a loaf of bread.

Then there is moral corruption. There was a time if a man made a deal or gave his word, it meant something. That is not true today. You could have your word notarized, or even homogenized, and it still would mean nothing. Why moral corruption?

As we watch television, we see the increase in violence. Violence is everywhere. Mankind has become stressed and angry. There is child abuse, gang terror, and even road rage. There has been a great increase in gun purchases. We all live in fear.

When we go to an airport to board an airplane, it takes us a long time to board the airplane. Why are we living in fear of terrorism? We live in a sick, violent society.

Another sign from the days of Noah is an increase in the arts and industry. The Bible declares that in the last days we will be able to number every single person and know exactly where they are and how they live. That is true today. It is easy to see how technology has increased.

Look at the cell phone. In some places in Japan, they do not use money any longer. Their cell phone pays for everything. If you ever go on a flight, you will look stupid holding a ticket. Most of the people have their ticket on their cell phones.

This is all part of the globalist's plan. Their plan is for a One World government, One World currency, and One World dictator. We are moving toward the end, yet the church is unaware and is once again silent.

Let me illustrate what is happening today. Has anybody taken a cruise? They might have five thousand crew and passengers. Fifteen hundred are the crew and the rest are vacationers. The passengers are sitting out in the sun and listening to Calypso music. They are dipping themselves in the pool and having fun. The whole ship is being run by the crew: they have the microphones, the keys, and the very helm to steer any way they wish. The United States is the same way.

Today, the media is controlling what is important and true. We call it fake news. More than 50 percent of America is watching it and believing it. They have the controls and are in charge of the technology. We in the church sing another song or hear another sermon, and the world is going to hell in a handbasket.

We are moving toward a globalist society. Once President Trump is gone, the globalists will have another window of opportunity to control it all. It does not matter if you are a Republican or Democrat—they are all globalists.

The Bible says in the "Last Days" people will have children without the bond of marriage. Everybody today is living together, and it is accepted. When I first started in the ministry and someone was living together, I would say, "I am so sorry, but you cannot teach Sunday school. Also, you cannot sing in the choir." "Why?" "Because you are setting a poor example of Jesus Christ." "Oh, do not be judgmental, pastor! Do not be judge and the executioner." "I am not being judgmental. I am being biblical. That is what the Bible calls a sin. You cannot allow that behavior in the leadership of the church." I will tell you that, 90 percent of the churches today say that it is acceptable. When I pastored in Tampa, I did several weddings a year. I cannot tell you the last time I did a wedding. Marriage is not important today. The government rewards women who have children without being married. Why?

A church member went to a Christian school from kindergarten to college. In Christian college, she met and married a Christian man. While they were engaged, they went to a Christian friend's wedding. Some of their

Christian friends came over to them and asked, "Are you guys engaged?" They said, "Yes." "Oh, are you both living together?" And they answered, "No, we are waiting until we get married." Their friends were astonished and asked, "What's wrong with you?"

Christians are making fun of other Christians for being pure. There is something wrong today if you are ridiculed for obeying Jesus Christ! We are raising a society that will not obey the commandments of God. Today, kids do not listen to their teachers, police, or even their parents. We are living In the "Days of Noah." Jesus is coming soon.

Let me close this chapter by comparing the Ark of Noah and our salvation in Jesus Christ. The Ark of Noah is a type (an Old Testament picture of a person or event in the New Testament) of Christ.

On Noah's Ark, there was only one door. Jesus is the truth and the only way to heaven.

Noah invited all the world aboard. Noah preached faithfully for over 120 years. He offered grace and mercy to all who would believe and enter the Ark.

The cross of Christ and the Ark were both made of wood. The cross and the Ark took the punishment for our sins. The flood shows us how God hates sin and yet loves the sinner. The Ark also shows us that God always gives us a way to escape judgment.

How is the flood like our day today? At the time of Noah, all the world was as one without God. The world was full of violence and immorality. Like today, the world would not obey or follow and was cursed by God.

Today the world is moving to a One World government (Globalism). If you watch the news today, all you see is murder, violence, and immorality. The world is looking for help but not including God.

THIRD GREAT EVENT

Tower of Babel – Globalism and the One World

Turn to Genesis 10 as we look at the third Great Event that precedes the second coming of Christ. The third Great Event we see in Genesis is like our day today—the Tower of Babel and the confusion of the languages. I believe the first 12 chapters of Scripture tell us how it is going to be in the last days. Why do we believe and teach these events? This belief comes from the very mouth of the Lord Jesus who said, "As the days of Noah, so shall it be in the days of the coming of the son of man."

Review

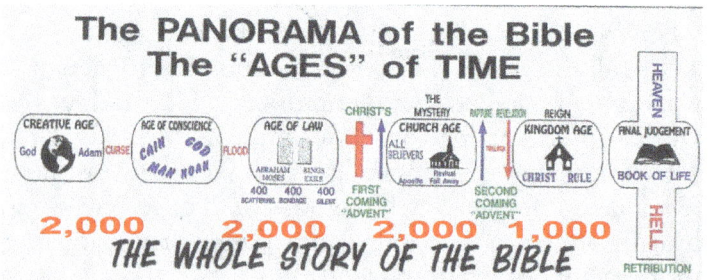

Look at this chart that covers from creation to the end of time. The world as we know it is only six thousand years old. God created with age. Look in the first chapter for more about this timeline.

Here is how God divides this span of time. From the time of creation to the time of the flood is two thousand years. From the time of the flood to the time of Christ—how long? 1,993 years, seven years short of the two thousand years. Remember, Jesus got cut off (crucified) at age thirty-three—and we will finish this time period during the seven-year tribulation period, which is yet to come. Then from the time of Christ and the beginning of the church in Acts 1 to where we are today has been almost two thousand years. Sometime near the year 2033, it will be two thousand years.

Am I saying Jesus is coming in the year 2033? No! We must remember that the calendar we use today has never been correct. It has been updated, corrected, and edited too many times to count. Our calendar may not be perfect, but it is close.

I want you to see that the seven days of creation and the seven thousand years of mankind are similar. I believe God was giving us a clue to His second coming. God was showing us that we will labor for six thousand years like the first six days of creation. Then we will rest with God for a thousand years. Remember, on the seventh day God rested. Our millennial rest for a thousand years is yet to come.

This is why evolution is so wrong. Scientists tell us how the world is billions and billions of years old. Even some Christians believe this. No! God created the world "with age." Remember, we do not follow man's wisdom but the Word of God.

In Matthew 24, Jesus said, "When you see things happening as in the days of Noah, my time of coming is near." How was it in those days? Number one, they started denying the existence of God. We live in a day if you tell someone you believe in God you are ridiculed or laughed at. Many think that a belief in God is for the uneducated. The Bible says that only a fool would say in his heart there is no God.

Secondly, there will be conflict and wars throughout the world. Every time you turn the TV on you hear of another conflict or trouble spot in the world. It is happening today. Recently, I was in a motel, and on the television, they were talking about what was happening in Iran, and then they were reporting, "Saudi Arabia just got bombed." I said to my wife, "Did you hear that?" I do not believe people realize the seriousness of the world situation. We are living in a very precarious world. The people in the White House and Congress understand, but no one wants to tell the truth. We must always remember this world is not our home. Do not allow the stress of this world to overcome us. We are more than conquerors through Christ.

And then thirdly, in the last days, the world will all be united as one. It is called the New World Order. Most of our politicians and world leaders are "Globalists." We all wish for peace and unity, but we will never have unity without Jesus Christ. As long as we live in this sinful and selfish world, we can never be unified.

As we approach these last days there will be an attack against the family. For the first time in human history, more babies are born outside of marriage by single mothers than by a loving family with a mother and father. I imagine most of you have somebody in your family who is "living together." Most of society says, Well, everybody's doing it. That's correct. And the Bible says, When you hear everybody doing it, that is when Jesus is coming.

We have discovered a power in these last 150 years that can destroy the entire world. The discovery of atomic power, and the radiation it gives off is described in 2 Peter 3. These verses speak of elements burning and melting with a great noise. Why use the word elements? Elements are atoms, again the Bible is ahead of the scientist using the word elements two thousand years before we found that elements even existed.

> But the day of the Lord will come as a thief in the night; in the which the heavens shall pass away with a *great noise*, and the *elements shall melt* with fervent heat, the earth also and the works that are therein shall be *burned up*. Seeing then that all these things shall be *dissolved*, what manner of persons ought ye to be in all holy conversation and godliness, Looking for and hasting unto the coming of the day of God, wherein the *heavens being on fire* shall be dissolved, and the elements shall melt with fervent heat? – 2 Peter 3:10–12

It's not always been here. The destruction that is mentioned in this passage shows that the world will be *destroyed by the elements* and a *fire burning*. I'm telling you; we're living in that time today.

In the last days, there will also be an increase in speed and knowledge and, of course, education. We are living in a day of daily discoveries and scientific marvels. More people are educated and are getting a college education than ever before. These same educated people think they know more than God. The Bible also says in 2 Peter 3:3–4 that "there shall come in the last days scoffers, walking after their own lusts, And saying, Where is the promise of his coming? for since the fathers fell asleep, all things continue as they were from the beginning of creation." So, shall it be in the last days. Unfortunately, we are destroying the foundations that our civilized world has been built upon.

Two men

I think sometimes we get confused over the second coming of Christ. Let me fill you in on the facts! It could happen today. Believers today all agree that the Lord Jesus was crucified on a cross, He was in the tomb for three days, on the third day He rose from the dead, and He was alive for forty days. But that is not all—He promised to return again, to judge and end the world. This is called the second coming of Christ. Look with me in Acts 1

> And when he had spoken these things, while they beheld, *he was taken up; and a cloud* received him out of their sight. And while they looked stedfastly toward heaven as he went up, behold, *two men stood by them* in white apparel; Which also said, Ye men of Galilee, why stand ye gazing up into heaven? This same Jesus, which is taken up from you into heaven, shall so come in like manner as ye have seen him go into heaven.
> – Acts 1:9–11

This event is called the ascension of Jesus Christ, which occurred forty days after the resurrection of Christ.

There were two witnesses standing with Jesus. I believe those two witnesses were Moses and Elijah. The Bible says that two men stood there with Jesus, not angels. This is not the first time Moses and Elijah stood with Jesus. Remember, Moses and Elijah were there when Jesus began his ministry: they appeared with Jesus on the Mount of Transfiguration.

After Jesus' death, He was placed in a tomb for three days. The Bible says that after His resurrection two men stood by the tomb's door.

> Now upon the first day of the week, very early in the morning, they came unto the sepulchre,

> bringing the spices which they had prepared, and certain others with them. And they found the stone rolled away from the sepulchre. And they entered in, and found not the body of the Lord Jesus. And it came to pass, as they were much perplexed thereabout, behold, *two men stood by them* in shining garments. – Luke 24:1–4

It does not mention them by name, but I believe Moses and Elijah announced every significant event in Jesus' ministry. Moses and Elijah, I believe, were these two men at the tomb. I believe that it was Moses and Elijah, once again, announcing the great events of the Lord Jesus.

Moses and Elijah were announcing His ministry at the Mount of Transfiguration, they were announcing his resurrection and power over death at the Tomb, and I believe in Acts 1 they were announcing His ascension into heaven here at the Mount of Olives.

Those two men spoke to the 120 followers of Jesus and said, "This same Jesus who you saw going into heaven *shall likewise come in the same manner.*" Jesus ascended into heaven and He has been sitting at the right hand of the Father for two thousand years.

In Revelation 11 these two witnesses will announce the second coming of Christ.

> And I will give power unto my two witnesses, and they shall prophesy a thousand two hundred and threescore days, clothed in sackcloth. These are the two olive trees, and the two candlesticks standing before the God of the earth. And if any man will hurt them, fire proceedeth out of their mouth, and devoureth their enemies: and if any man will hurt them, he must in this manner be killed. These have power to shut heaven, that it rain not in the days of their prophecy: and have power over waters to turn them to blood, and to

smite the earth with all plagues, as often as they will. And when they shall have finished their testimony, the beast that ascendeth out of the bottomless pit shall make war against them, and shall overcome them, and kill them. And their dead bodies shall lie in the street of the great city, which spiritually is called Sodom and Egypt, where also our Lord was crucified. And they of the people and kindreds and tongues and nations shall see their dead bodies three days and an half, and shall not suffer their dead bodies to be put in graves. – Revelation 11:3–9

But the Bible says that He is coming back the same way He ascended. He went up in the clouds and He will come back in the clouds. Jesus' second coming is described in 1 Thessalonians 4,

> But I would not have you to be ignorant, brethren, concerning them which are asleep, that ye sorrow not, even as others which have no hope. For if we believe that Jesus died and rose again, even so them also which sleep in Jesus will God bring with him. For this we say unto you by the word of the Lord, that we which are alive and remain unto the coming of the Lord shall not prevent them which are asleep. For the Lord himself shall descend from heaven with a shout, with the voice of the archangel, and with the trump of God: and the dead in Christ shall rise first: Then we which are alive and remain shall be *caught up together with them in the clouds,* to meet the Lord in the air: and so shall we ever be with the Lord. Wherefore comfort one another with these words.
> – 1 Thessalonians 4:13–18

The second coming of Jesus will occur in two separate appearances. He will come again first in the clouds. At this time Jesus will call His church to "Come up hither." In Revelation 4:1 Jesus says, "Come up hither." We call this appearing the "rapture." The word *rapture* comes from an English phrase that means "to be caught by surprise." We do not use that kind of language, but sometimes if you're watching an English movie, you'll hear a person say, "Oh, rapture. Oh, joy." They are expressing their astonishment.

The Bible says in 1 Thessalonians 4:16 that "the dead in Christ shall rise first." That means all the graves of the saved believers will be emptied and their corrupted bodies will be transformed into a new glorified body and join Jesus in the clouds. Today when we bury our loved ones we bury their bodies, not their souls. Their souls go to be with Jesus. But at the second coming of Christ, Jesus will open up the graves and they will be given a new body in a twinkling of an eye.

At the very same moment, all of the saved believers who are alive will also be "caught up" to be with Jesus. These two simultaneous events are both called the "rapture." 1 Corinthians 15:51–52 says we shall "all be changed" at the time of Jesus' return. This mortal will put on immortality. This corruptible shall be put on incorruptible, and so shall we ever be with the Lord. Amen!

Tribulation: rapture and revelation

After the rapture, the seven-year tribulation occurs. The rapture triggers the tribulation events. The rapture starts the clock up again to complete the seven years that were stopped at the death of Jesus. This last seven years is called the "tribulation period."

The world has never seen what is going to happen. Some people would rather die than wake up the next morning during the tribulation. The Bible says there will be great starvation. In fact, starvation is so bad, the antichrist begins a numbering system that will ration out food for all. This food rationing will be done militaristically and it will take a day's salary to buy a loaf of bread (Revelation 6:6). The antichrist will be hailed and lifted up with praise. People will say, "We would not have food to eat without him [antichrist] and will worship him as a god."

After the seven-year tribulation period, Jesus comes back as King of Kings and Lord of Lords to claim His throne that was offered to Him at the triumphal entry into the city of Jerusalem. This is the second phase of the second coming of Jesus. This return is called the "Revelation" of Jesus. Jesus comes *with* His resurrected saints, riding on a white horse, and is called the King of Kings.

In the first phase, the rapture, Jesus comes *for* His church. He resurrects and transforms His dead (those who have died and were saved) and alive saints' bodies (those who are saved now) and takes them home with Him. Then the seven-year tribulation period. Then occurs the second phase of His coming, called the "Revelation of Jesus Christ." Jesus comes and places His foot on the Mount of Olives. He claims Jerusalem as His kingdom's home. When this happens, a great earthquake occurs and splits the capital of Jerusalem into pieces. He will recreate the heavens and the earth. We will then live with Jesus Christ as our king for a thousand years.

I've been to Israel five times. When you go down from the Mount of Olives, you go straight down to the Garden of Gethsemane, where Jesus prayed. When you leave the garden, you must go straight up. At the top of the other side of the valley is the great Temple. What is this Valley? It's a fault line. It's the biggest fault line in Israel. Now, get this: Jesus comes back, His foot hits the Mount of Olives and an earthquake occurs. The Bible says that in this earthquake, one-third of the world is killed in one instance. He comes over and claims ownership of the Temple Mount. Jesus now announces to all that He is the King of Kings and Lord of Lords.

So, we now know the two great phases of the second coming of Jesus. First, the rapture, and seven years later, the revelation.

Review

There are certain things that are going to precede His second coming. Number one is a denying of the creation and existence of God. This began 150 years ago with the theory and philosophy of evolution. God created the universe and our world with age. He did not create Adam as a baby or a plant as a seed. God certainly had the chicken come before the egg. So, all of His creation appears to be billions of years old. It was created old! Every scientist I talked to—and I've talked to dozens—acts like, "Huh? I never thought of that. No wonder everything seems to have age." Yes, it was created with age, but the creation occurred only six thousand years ago.

Why do I believe that? First, the Bible says it and I believe it. But the universe shows the handy work of a supreme being. Secondly, Jesus describes creation and declares creation as true. In fact, Jesus was the one who created all the universe. Praise the Lord.

Great Event number two is the flood. There is great evidence of a worldwide flood. The flood also tells us that the last days will be like the days of Noah. Over the past four thousand years, the seven landmasses (continents) have separated. These landmasses are still moving. Most of them are moving up to an inch a year. Sometimes they get caught and the tension builds up and then all of a sudden, they move a distance and we call that an earthquake. We're living in a time some call the day of the earthquakes. Since 1990 there have been more earthquakes than ever in recorded history.

In my anthropology classes, we were taught that we can trace our lineage back to three different cultures and three different people groups. I raised my hand and read the same thing from the Bible. There were three sons of Noah who became three family units and three different cultures with three different languages. Shem, who went to Asia; Japheth, who went to Europe; and Ham, who went to Africa.

We see these three people groups in the Book of Acts. Peter was given the responsibility of opening the church to all three descendants of Noah and not just the Jewish nation. Peter was given the keys to these three kingdoms. I have seen artwork from the Louvre to the Vatican and even in Washington, D.C. and some of those sixteenth-century paintings are wonderful. How can you tell which saint or character is in the painting? If the saint is carrying a sword, it's Paul. Why? Because he wrote the sword of the spirit. If the saint is carrying keys, it is Peter. If there is a spear in the saint's side, it is Andrew. In every painting of Peter, guess how many keys are on the ring? Three—one for each son of Noah. Peter opened the Gospel to the three groups of people. The Gospel is not only for the Jews, but God so loved the world!

We also see the number three at the battle of Armageddon. The three kings: from the South, out of Africa; from the East, out of China and India; and from the North, out of Europe. All three uniting together against God in the battle of Armageddon. This idea of a united New World Order comes from the Tower of Babel.

The reason I am reviewing again is that these events are happening one after the other. These five events build upon one another. I want you to see and remember the antichrist's plan. Please do not be deceived!

The third Great Event

The third Great Event is the Tower of Babel. I am going to answer some questions you may have. First of all, where and when did nations and their languages begin? And where did the different religions come from? Yes, they all come to us from an event that occurred four thousand years ago.

The world would like all of us to be united in one united religion. The religion of the future is "tolerance" and "coexistence." This is how it was during the time of the Tower of Babel. The world had one leader (Nimrod), one religion (paganism), and one language.

Today, all the religions have the same source: they all stem from the Tower of Babel. It does not matter if it is Hinduism, Buddhism, Islam, and unfortunately even some Christian denominations—all stem from the Tower of Babel. The Catholic church has incorporated many of the rituals from the Tower of Babel.

These religions call their "gods" different names but all stem from the same gods of Babel. The gods of Babel are Baal and Ashtaroth. The male and female god and goddess. After the people of Babel were scattered, they gave their gods different names but all had the same source—Babel. Not only did they deny the True God, but they also disobeyed God by doing everything in their imagination: sin, crime, disease, and immorality.

On a trip to China in early 2019, my wife and I saw the birthplace of Buddha. The Chinese government spent hundreds of millions of dollars on this beautiful place. They showed how Buddha was birthed out of a lotus plant as a young child of the sun and moon god. There is this huge metal lotus tree, about three stories high, and then it opens up and—behold—there is baby Buddha, about 50 feet high and with his normal potbelly. Most religions can be traced back to the Tower of Babel and Nimrod himself. Any religion that makes man a god or has a mother and son deities is a false religion and had its beginnings in Babel.

The story of the Tower of Babel begins in the first part of Genesis. Genesis 10:1–10 tells us about the descendants of Noah and his three sons. The Tower of Babel begins with a character named Nimrod in verse 8. He was a descendant of Ham, who migrated toward Africa. Nimrod was a mighty hunter before the Lord and begins the Kingdom of Babel.

The Tower of Babel is described in Genesis 11. In verse 1, it says the whole earth is "one." They had one language and one speech. Now, it came to pass as they journeyed from the East and they found the plain of Shinar and there they dwelt. By the way, that is Iraq today. This is the reason Iran, Iraq, and Pakistan are so important today. That is also where the Garden of Eden was located. You may ask, "How do we know that?" There are two rivers mentioned in Eden, the river Tigris, and the river Euphrates. These two rivers are found in those three lands.

Why is this area so important? Noah built his Ark here. Abraham comes from Ur near Babylon. This is where Jonah went and preached to the people of Nineveh. This is where Daniel was in the lion's den. Then this is where three Hebrew children were thrown into the fiery furnace. So, when we talk about this area, Babylon is important. This area is where it all began, and it is where all the world will end!

The area of Babel and these three countries is where many of the Bible prophecies occur. This is also where the wise men came from. Why have we not heard for two thousand years about Iran or Iraq or Syria, yet now they are in the news every night? Jesus said where it all began is where it will all end.

> And they said to one another, Go to, let us make brick, and burn them thoroughly. And they had brick for stone, and slime had they for morter. And they said, Go to, let us build us a city and a tower, whose top may reach unto the heaven; and let us make us a name, lest we be scattered abroad upon the face of the whole earth. – Genesis 11:3–4
>
> And the Lord came down to see the city and the tower, which the children of men builded. And the Lord said, Behold, the people is one, and they have all one language; and this they all begin to do: and now nothing with will be restrained from them, which they have imagined to do. – Genesis 11:5–6

God had told the people to be scattered, for the landmasses were moving apart.

> Go to, let us go down, and there confound their language, that they may not understand one another's speech. So the Lord scattered them abroad from thence upon the face of all the earth: and they left off to build the city. Therefore is the name of it called Babel; because the Lord did there confound the language of all the earth: and from thence did the Lord scatter them abroad upon the face of all the earth. – Genesis 11:7–9

Babel means confusion. What do you tell somebody if they're talking foolishness? They are babbling. This is where the word comes from.

Gods and goddesses

Now, here is where the story of Nimrod begins and ends. We found this in the archives and in the artifacts from that land. This is what he looked like. He was a mighty hunter. He was the son of Cush. Cush was the son of Ham, Noah's son. Nimrod married his mother, Semiramis, who is known as Ishtar in Babylon and Isis in Egypt. She was worshipped as Venus in Rome and Aphrodite in Greece. She was also called Diana—the great fertility goddess of the Ephesians. The Old Testament Canaanites called this fertility goddess Ashteroth. Baal (Nimrod) was her male companion (Judges 2:12; 3:7; 1 Kings 18:19; 2 Kings 21:7). She was called the Queen of Heaven.

This began the worldwide worship of male and female gods who brought fertility. This worship of mother and child spread throughout the known world, so they are known by different names throughout the world. Ancient Germans worshipped the virgin Hertha and her child who she always

carried. Scandinavians called her Disa and pictured her with a small child. To the Egyptians, she and her son are known as Isis with the infant Osiris seated on his mother's lap. In India, the worship of mother and child continued as Devaki and Krishna.

Semiramis was both Nimrod's wife and mother. She was worshiped as the "mother of god" and as a "fertility goddess." Nimrod is called the "sun god" and Semiramis is called the "moon goddess." They were both stumbling blocks for the Jews throughout the Old Testament. The Prophet Jeremiah prophesied about the worship of this goddess, Ashtaroth.

Jeremiah 7:18 and 44:19 both refer to the queen of heaven:

> The women knead their dough, to make cakes to the queen of heaven, and to pour out drink offerings unto other gods, that they may provoke me to anger. – Jeremiah 7:18

> And when we burned incense to the queen of heaven, and poured out drink offerings unto her, did we make her cakes to worship her, and pour out drink offerings unto her, without our men? – Jeremiah 44:19

In every religion throughout the world and written in history, there is a female and a male god and goddess. In Canaan, the male god, Baal, and the female god, Ashtaroth. We also celebrate and commemorate these two gods right here in America. We call it Christmas and Easter. Christmas is the sun god. That is why the date is December 25 when we thought the days were getting shorter. They would sacrifice a virgin and ask their gods to bring back the sun. How do you like that? A virgin woman? If their gods accepted the sacrifice, the days would get longer. The virgin who was killed on that day was changed to the Virgin Mary. By December 25, they noticed the days were getting longer and would have a winter celebration. Christmas is based on the winter solstice which falls just a few days before Christmas.

The pagans called it a celebration of the sun god. The Catholic Church tried to assimilate their culture and their holidays by changing it to fit the Catholic religion. The Catholics changed the sun god to the Son of God. They called it Christmas.

During the spring equinox, the pagans celebrated fertility with green grass, eggs, and bunnies. All are symbols of fertility. The Catholic Church assimilated it once again and called it "Easter" or Ashtaroth. Easter also is based on the first moon of spring and not the Jewish Passover. It is a spring celebration to mother earth, Semiramis. Jesus was not resurrected at Easter. He was resurrected after the Passover, not during the spring equinox. Yes, it was springtime, but it's not Easter.

Nimrod began the worship of the zodiac, which we call astrology. Man began to name the stars and began to worship them as gods. How foolish is the worship of stars and planets? Have you ever seen a constellation like Taurus the Bull, which does not look anything like a bull, or Aries, which does not look anything like a ram? All of the zodiac figures look nothing like their names.

People still foolishly look daily at the newspaper to see their horoscope. Where did it come from? It came from Nimrod. He started astrology.

Recently, the news reported a big fire in the Notre Dame Cathedral. When I visited the Cathedral in Paris France, I was astonished to see that the south wall had a stained glass window that depicted the Zodiac. When I turned to the north wall, its stained glass window depicted the 12 stages of Christ's life. It was beautiful! What had happened? I later learned that the south wall was completed centuries after the north wall. The south wall was finished during the black period of the Catholic Church. Once again, the Catholic Church was delving into the teachings of the Tower of Babel.

We also see sun worship in the Catholic communion service. The Catholics believe the communion wafer, round in the shape of the sun, becomes the essence of god. This is called "transubstantiation." The ancient Egyptians also used a wafer to represent god. It was round like their sun-god, and Egyptian priests would put their sun-god into a wafer. The Catholics keep the wafer in a canister called a monstrance (the device where the wafer is placed when it is being adored) it is also shaped like a *sunburst*. This is a symbol of *Baal*, which goes all the way back to Nimrod.

So, like the Catholics, the Protestants have incorporated the idea of Easter and Christmas. Everybody is bowing down to Baal and to Ashtaroth. Nothing's new. It all goes back to the Tower of Babel. In almost every book in the Old Testament, the Jews would stray from God's commandments and statues to follow the false god Baal and his spouse Ashtaroth.

Sexual immorality

The Jews lived in a primarily agricultural community. They were mostly farmers, so they needed crops and they needed water. Instead of trusting the God of Abraham, they would sacrifice to the fertility gods Baal and Ashtoreth. Now, I don't want to be too crude here, but it was their belief that if Baal had intercourse with his mother Ashtoreth and it was fruitful, there was plenty of rain. If they did not have intercourse, there was no rain. The way to encourage the gods to be "fruitful" was to engage in sexual immorality.

In the Old Testament, when Moses came down from the Mount with the Ten Commandments, the Jewish people were all worshipping Baal and Ashtaroth. They were dancing around it naked, and Moses said, "Who is on the Lord's side? Let him come unto me" (Exodus 32:26).

When you look through Scripture, every culture and every people group has a male god and a female god. We see it in the Greek and Roman cultures. In Scripture, we read how the pagans worshipped Diana, Venus, Cupid, Mars, and Jupiter. All of these gods have their roots in the Tower of Babel and Nimrod and Semiramis.

In Genesis 10:8–9, Nimrod is called the mighty hunter. He becomes a leader in Babylon and builds the Tower of Babel. He is worshipped as a god and his mother as the "mother of god." Here are three pictures of mother and son gods. The far-right picture is of Mary and Jesus—can you see a difference? No. That is so sad.

The Catholic Church worships a dead Jesus on the cross (Crucifix) or a baby Jesus on the lap of his mother Mary. In the Orthodox churches, pictures or crosses become "icons" and are believed to hold holy power or good luck.

There is a beautiful Greek Orthodox church in Tarpon Springs, Florida, one of the most beautiful churches in Florida. All Greek Orthodox churches and Russian Orthodox churches are similar to the Jewish beliefs and customs. All of their sanctuaries are designed in three sections, just like the Jewish Temple.

They have a congregational area, a Holy place that only priests are allowed to occupy, and then a veil or a screened separation, adorned with picture icons. Behind this screen is the Holy of Holies where only the orthodox High Priest can enter.

Now, on every veil or screen, there is always this picture, the large mother Mary, the little child Jesus. In the church in Tarpon Springs, Florida, there is a lady who follows after you. Why? So in case you kiss the icons she can use Windex and a little rag to keep the icon clean. They even have a glass shield in front of the icon with a hole in the glass. Why a hole? For you to put in jewelry or money between the glass and the picture. The more you kiss or the more you give, the more good luck you have. I thanked her and said it would not be necessary—I only kiss and give jewelry to my wife—but this does bring me good luck! This is all idol worship and can be traced back to the Tower of Babel. Only God determines what is holy or not holy.

When I was in the Vatican, right outside the beautiful Sistine Chapel they have a tapestry that is probably 50 feet long by 40 feet high. This tapestry is called the Coronation of Mary, the Mother of God. In the picture, we see God the Father, the  Holy Spirit, and the Son, Jesus, bowing down to Mary, and Mary hailed as the Queen of Heaven. This is blasphemy: Mary would never want to be elevated to be equal or above God! I understand that the Catholic Church incorporated pagan doctrines to be able to reach the pagan people, but when incorporating beliefs, we should never allow idol worship.

The Tower of Babel

The Tower of Babel ceased to exist, but we find other ziggurats in Egypt. They were built in honor of Ra, the male sun god, and Isis, the female moon goddess.

Now, the Tower of Babel had seven levels.[4] Why? One for each of the planets they could see, which was seven planets. They knew there were seven days in a week, and this was their attempt to go to God by a works salvation.

They did not want to go through the blood sacrifice in order to worship God. They did not want to be like Abel or Noah and sacrifice a lamb. Nimrod said we can get to heaven our own way. We do not need to obey God. We are smart enough all by ourselves. We have the technology, we have everything we need, we do not need God.

God allowed them to build their ziggurat. And when they finally got to the seventh level, God came down and leveled it. By the way, Saddam Hussein had rebuilt the Tower of Babel. It has become a tourist stop. Many of the young people in Iraq are married at the Tower of Babel. Why did they build seven tiers or levels? They knew it was God's number of creation.

Babel means confusion and that is exactly what God did. He confused their languages. The people of Babel wanted to live and worship as they pleased. They wanted nothing to do with any rules or doctrines to follow. They said, "We want one language and one world without interference by God!"

Now, remember that all the landmasses were together as one big puzzle. All neatly fitted together. Each of these landmasses is called a continent or plate. They were all pushed together. The plates are separated on lines called fault lines. These plates are always moving and sliding away from each other. When a landmass gets stuck and then moves suddenly this is called an earthquake.

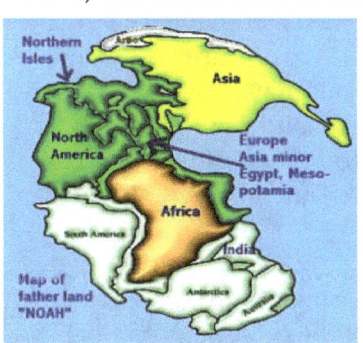

God told the descendants of Noah to go, spread out, and replenish the entire world (Genesis 8:17, 9:1–7). He knew that soon the landmasses would be separating and replaced by the seven major oceans. God knew if they did not spread out quickly over all the landmasses, the floodwaters would be receded and it would be too late.

History tells us it would take many years before people could travel by boat across an ocean and connect with other people. Now was the only time to move! They said no and became disobedient to God's Word. "We are going to do it our own way." God said, "If you stay here, you'll die."

In Genesis 11:7 God speaks as a united Trinitarian voice: "Let us go down, and there confound their language, that they may not understand one another's speech." People grouped themselves together by speech and possibly by shade of skin and separated into tribes and families. Let us never forget there was only one race. It all goes back to Adam. Yes, Noah had three sons, but we all come from the same genetic pool as Adam and Eve. We are all brothers and sisters.

I think the church of God is making a tremendous mistake when we talk about black churches and white churches. I realize there are cultural differences, but these differences should make us stronger. The greatest testimony to the world of the love of Christ is to have the doors of our churches open and have Hispanics, Native Americans, African Americans, and Caucasians all walking out hand in hand. United together in Christ. That is the way it is supposed to be. That's the way Jesus wanted it to be.

History and archeology show us that all the descendants of Noah broke into three people groups and aligned themselves along the lines of the three sons of Noah. We will see these three people groups uniting again in the last days as the three kings who war against God in the Valley of Megiddo.

Dr. Kevin M. Ahrens

Globalism: 12 stars

What does all this have to do with the last days? What we see happening over the past 150 years is a movement toward globalism. Just like in Babel, we want to be united without God or His Word. The last several presidents have all been globalists. Most of the elected officials have all been globalist. This political slant crosses party lines and has been the demise of our country over the past several decades.

We have seen our steel mills and other large corporations move out of our country. Our military has been forced to fight under a United Nations flag and not an American flag. We are getting to a place where everybody wants to use one language, one monetary system, and follow one leader, who will move this world forward. Hold on—one money, one language, one people. We are reviving the spirit of Babel. The only leader we should follow is King Jesus Christ.

This recent globalist thinking began with President George Bush, Sr., some forty years ago. Each president following continued this globalist movement, no matter which party they were affiliated with. President Donald Trump had broken this globalist cycle. It was good for our economy, but the other elected globalists will not go away easily.

The world is united together as never before The media and movies have brought all the cultures and philosophies together. The world is also connected by satellites. Over in Europe all the nations united together and formed the European Common Union, ECU. When I first went to Europe some thirty years ago, you had to exchange money in every different country. Now all European nations use the euro as their monetary currency.

The Bushes moved our country to become like Europe and had us join NAFTA. We became one united region with all South and North America and Canada united as one. It almost destroyed our country.

Recently, Great Britain pulled out of their union (Brexit). This opposition, along with President Trump, is slowing up the antichrist's global plans. God is raising up some people in Britain, and strong leaders like President Trump, who are saying no to globalism. Let me show a connection between the euro and Nimrod's Tower of Babel.

The globalist's goal is for the world to unite together as one nation, one people, one language, one money, and one leader. The above right picture was issued by the European Union, showing the Tower of Babel and carrying the slogan: "Many tongues, one voice." There is a crane in the background showing the rebuilding of the tower. Above the Tower of Babel, you can see 12 Eurostars, but they are inverted, as in witchcraft, with the central points downward. This poster promotes the European Common Market, showing the Tower of Babel surrounded by 12 stars. They were asked, Why the Tower of Babel? Because our history goes back to the Tower of Babel.

Look at the picture on the left. This is a euro and we see it also has a picture of a woman called Europa, surrounded by 12 Eurostars. Why are there are 12 stars? The Book of Revelation says the harlot is surrounded by 12 stars. Europa is called the woman of the apocalypse crowned with 12 stars as mentioned in Revelation 17. In mythology, Europa, which is where Europe gets her name, is the Phoenician princess who was abducted and raped by the king of the gods, Zeus.

The Bible predicts in the last days the Roman Empire would be reunited and be led by a woman with 12 stars.

> And there appeared a great wonder in heaven; a *woman clothed with the sun, and the moon* under her feet, and upon her head a crown of *twelve stars*: And *she being with child* cried, travailing in birth, and pained to be delivered. And there appeared another wonder in heaven; and behold a great red dragon, having seven heads and ten horns, and seven crowns upon his heads. – Revelation 12:1–3

This is the European Union flag. Many of our young men and women are fighting underneath this flag or a United Nations flag, instead of the United States flag. All of it is in prophecy. The former secretary-general of the Council of Europe, Léon Marchal, affirmed that the stars are those of "the woman of the Apocalypse." It is the *corona stellarum duodecim* (the crown of the twelve stars) of the woman of the Apocalypse. Although this woman represents Israel, the Catholic Church has always claimed that she represents the Virgin Mary, "the Mother of God."[5]

The European Common Union was started in 1957 with Belgian Paul-Henri Charles Spaak as president. Spaak said, "What we want is a man of sufficient stature to hold the allegiance of all people, and to lift us out of the economic morass into which we are sinking. Send us such a man, and be he god or devil, we will receive him."[6]

Now, look at this picture. Here is England's Prime Minister Tony Blair in 2014 signing the European Union's constitution. They met at the Vatican. This is in a hallway, right outside the Sistine Chapel. The signers are surrounded by images of past popes. What do you see in front of them on the table? 12 Eurostars.

Why did they sign the European Market Unification at the Vatican? Why not another place? They answered this question when Tony Blair and the other European leaders went to the roof of the Vatican with the pope. After the signing of the constitution, as they stood on the roof, they all held hands and said, Today the European Market is now reunited. We are the revived Roman Empire spoken of in the Bible. Did you hear about that in the news? No! Tony Blair converted to Catholicism after this event.

The church today

I was raised Roman Catholic. Since my conversion to Christ, I have studied much about Catholicism. I have helped with Catholic funerals and have performed several weddings in the Catholic Church. Most of my extended family are Catholic, but they are coming to know Christ as their Savior.

The Catholic Church took over the Roman Empire in the fourth century. The Roman emperor was replaced by a Roman pope. Unfortunately, they incorporated much of Roman paganism. The Bible prophesied in the Book of Daniel that the Roman Empire will be restored in the last days. Many theologians today believe the European Union is a fulfillment of this prophecy.[7]

The Bible also prophesied that in the last days the world would be like Babel.[8] The world would be united as one religion, one government, one economy. The Bible says in the last days even the churches would follow the antichrist. The Bible says God will send mankind a strong delusion that they would believe a lie. It is happening in the churches today and many do not see it.

> Even him, whose coming is after the working of Satan with all power and signs and lying wonders, And with all deceivableness of unrighteousness in them that perish; because they received not the love of the truth, that they might be saved. And for this cause God shall send them strong delusion, that they should believe a lie: That they all might be damned who believed not the truth, but had pleasure in unrighteousness. – 2 Thessalonians 2:9-12

The gospel of tolerance is being pushed and preached every Sunday in the pulpits today. They call us radicals for believing the Bible literally. In many churches, the New Age Movement is coming and eroding the faith of believers, which is apostasy.

Churches are closing and others are declining weekly. Some of the big churches are staying open, but they are alive because they are compromising on God's truth. Their pulpits are tickling people's ears and they are not preaching the Gospel. My children went to Christian schools, but almost every one of those Christian schools is closed now. The Bible states that the "last days church" will be lukewarm, compromising, and lazy. The Bible calls it the church of Laodicea.

Religious tolerance

Pope Francis says, "The Lord has redeemed us all, all of us, with the blood of Christ. All of us, not just Catholics, everyone, even atheists."[9] This goes along with the teaching from the Tower of Babel. This pope is a false prophet who is being used by the antichrist to unite all religions.

Every time this pope travels, he travels with the Jewish rabbi and with a Muslim leader, calling them his brothers. Recently, the pope went to the Holy Lands with his "friends." He told the crowd on the Temple Mount, Let this place be for all the religions of the world to unity all together as brothers.

In Revelation 11 the Scripture says that the Temple will be rebuilt and used by the antichrist to unite all religions together. He will then call for him to be worshipped in the Temple.

In this Temple, Moses and Elijah appear to announce the coming of the Messiah. They have always announced Jesus' greatest events. The two witnesses come and take ownership of the Temple by measuring the Temple. Later they are killed and everyone in the world will see their bodies being killed and held in state for three days. God will raise the two witnesses from the dead and resurrect them to heaven. This is where the antichrist will show the world who he really is and demand to be worshipped.

How is the Tower of Babel a sign of the second coming of Christ? The Tower of Babel was built in the area around Iraq, Iran, and Syria. We hear on the news every night of the fighting in those three nations. They are fighting with the whole world and also with each other. Each nation feels they are the real descendants of Babel and should be in charge of this whole area.

How is Babel like us today? First, many people today are calling for a religion of tolerance. They say, "It does not matter what you believe. Why can't you Christians be more tolerant?" You might think the idea of tolerance is good and you would be wrong.

Christianity is not a tolerant religion. Jesus went into the Temple and turned over the money tables. John the Baptist said, "Ye are of your father the devil" (John 8:44). He was talking to the Jews. Jesus said there was one way, only one way. Tolerance is the religion of the devil, which is what we see happening today.

In fact, even the Catholic Church is pushing for tolerance. Pope Francis has repeatedly said that everybody is going to heaven—even the atheist. The new pope travels with a Jewish and Muslim religious leader to emphasize that we all worship the same God. Here is the truth: we are all going to hell and need forgiveness and redemption through Jesus Christ and His precious blood.

We are not tolerant, we are fundamentalist. We stand on the fundamentals of the Scripture. We must realize the world does not like us and never will. They killed Jesus. They will kill us also.

The church is being swallowed up in this thinking. Recently, a Southern Baptist leader led missionaries to help build a Muslim Mosque. He said it was to show the love of Christ.[10] God is not pleased!

All false religions come from the Tower of Babel. They follow the same lies of Satan that have been spread for over four thousand years. These religions all believe in making man into a god. This is also what evolution tells us: you are your own God.

By the way, many of these health and wealth preachers teach that we are all little gods. They say, "If you name it and claim it you have the power to make anything happen by your *own* power." When Benny Hinn comes over and says, "Be healed," he has the "power" to heal. In the Word of God, Peter said, "Jesus Christ maketh thee whole: arise, and make thy bed" (Acts 9:34). I remember Benny Hinn putting his arms out and blowing from his mouth on the audience, and they fell over and said they received the Holy Spirit. That is blasphemy! My friends, the only thing that he could do to knock over those people is with his own bad breath! It wasn't anything to do with the Holy Spirit.

In the church today, the idea of unity seems to be the key doctrine. The new mantra is, let us all come together. The salvation of man has been watered down and has excluded repentance.

Here is what we hear today: "Come join our church. There are no requirements and we accept everyone, no matter what lifestyle you follow. It does not matter what you are doing—there is no need for repentance. God is love and accepts everyone. Kumbaya. All you must do to be saved is come to Jesus just as you are. Ask Jesus to come into your heart. He does not expect you to change—He accepts us all." That is a lie! You say, "Wait a minute, pastor, is that not how we are saved?" Yes, but there must be repentance.

"If thou shalt confess with thy mouth the Lord Jesus, and believe in thine heart that God hath raised Him from the dead, thou shalt be saved" (Romans 10:9). You must come to a place where you realize you are lost without Christ.

Jesus illustrated this fact when He told of the two men who came to the Temple. One said, "God, have mercy on me, a sinner" (Luke 18:13). The other walked out and said, "What a good man I am. I am glad I am better than him." Jesus said that only one of those was redeemed, the one who repented. Oh, God! Be merciful to us.

Conclusion

How is this like the Tower of Babel? The people of Babel were very religious but lost. They wanted to get to heaven their own way and not God's. Their priorities were all wrong. Building this tower is more important than obeying God. They said, "Come as you are. It does not make any difference." They all listened to a human dynamic leader who was leading them astray. Nimrod, the antichrist.

The political elite of today is trying to build a New World Order. This order wants a One World government, one language, one religion of tolerance, and to follow one leader, the antichrist. They are more concerned about global warming than the dissolving of families and culture.

The antichrist will be handsome, articulate, loved, and will lead the world away from God. He will announce to the world, "We have all the answers to all the world's problems. We do not need God, church, or the Bible telling us what we should do. We are more enlightened than the religious Bible thumpers."

We are already moving toward a cashless society. Our country and the world are very close to bankruptcy. Our debt is growing exponentially daily. We are on the brink of a worldwide collapse. Out of this confusion will come the antichrist. He will bring the whole world together, either by force or persuasion. In the midst of this collapse, he will place the world in a system of monetary control. We will be numbered and not allowed to buy or sell without having an identity number (the Mark of the Beast).

In Japan, they are using cell phones instead of cash. Many people today pay all their bills online with their credit cards, which can be stolen. Identities can also be stolen. The solution is to put your identity number on or in your body. This will also help in security in travel. We can also track any illegal aliens in our country.

Most people know it as 666. It is the Mark of the Beast and comes from Revelation 13.

> And he causeth all, both small and great, rich and poor, free and bond, to receive a mark in their right hand, or in their foreheads: And that no man might buy or sell, save he that had the mark, or the name of the beast, or the number of his name. Here is wisdom. Let him that hath understanding count the number of the beast: for it is the number of a man; and his number is Six hundred threescore and six. – Revelation 13:16–18

The Mark of the Beast could be linked to our fingerprint or retina scan. Both are unique to each individual. Maybe the reason the Bible says that the mark will be on our hand and forehead is that is where your fingerprint and retina scan would be retrieved.

The antichrist may use a tiny micro-chip like veterinarians use on animals. This chip could also contain vital information and medical histories for instant care from a paramedic. This could also stop credit card fraud and check forgery.

You see how intelligent it is. There is already a tiny little chip on your credit card—this could be the beginning. That chip will be implanted underneath the back of the hand. When we go to the gas station, we would run our hand across a scanner. How easy. Nobody can steal it. Nobody can duplicate it. It could be the answer to all of our problems. But it will be the beginning of the end.

FOURTH GREAT EVENT

Sodom's Sin – Gay Agenda

I just want to preface my statements. There is something missing in Christianity today: it seems to me that nobody wants to talk about consequences anymore. Young people play in ball games and nobody wins. From Genesis to Revelation there is one word, one theme in every book. It can all be summed up in one word: "consequences." All the stories in Genesis show there is a consequence for sin. The Bible says in Romans 6:23 that the wages of sin is death. Galatians 6:7 says, "Be not deceived; God is not mocked: for whatsoever a man soweth, that shall he also reap."

Is it any wonder that in my era and lifetime, spanking became obsolete? My generation is also the generation of rebellion. Why? There was no consequence for misbehavior. There is not something wrong with Johnny, but rather, there something wrong with Johnny's parents or with Johnny's environment. Johnny's generation had never learned about the consequences of disobedience and grew up to be violent and rebellious. There is another word we see throughout Scripture and it is a similar word to consequence. It is the word "choices." Sin is a result of bad choices and there will be serious consequences for bad choices. This is just common sense! Kids today say, "Duh!"

If you go to Genesis, you will see how Adam and Eve were given a choice by God and they made a bad choice. They chose to disobey God. Then we see they and all of us suffered the consequences. Bad choices always lead to terrible consequences. The Bible is full of people who made good choices or bad choices. They received good or bad consequences. You would think that the world would learn from the consequences of their choices. The eternal truth we find in Scripture is that we are all sinners and seem to repeat the same mistakes others have made repeatedly.

Another problem with society today is that liberal theologians take the Word of God and make Swiss cheese out of it. So many people begin to doubt the Word of God and, again, make poor choices. Because of this doubt, many people struggle to define what is right or wrong. Someone said the way to have a successful life is to learn from your mistakes and learn also from other's mistakes. That may not be Scripture, but it makes sense.

Let us take a hard look at our churches and families today. Churches and families are dissolving, melting, or just plain dying. Our schools are failing to educate our children on the basics of life. We are raising half of our next generation as educated people that cannot make good decisions or the half that are deprived of making decisions at all because we failed to educate them with the skills to make good decisions. Most of society is sitting back just watching it fall away. Many feel there is nothing we can do. We just shake our heads in disbelief. This is very serious stuff we see happening, but we can make a difference! We can change! We need God's people to rise up and say enough is enough and take a stand on morality and against civil disobedience.

Review

Let us look back at our main passage, 2 Peter 3:3–4:

> "Knowing this first, that there shall come in the last days scoffers, walking after their own lusts, And saying, Where is the promise of his coming? for since the fathers fell asleep, all things continue as they were from the beginning of creation."

This is the theme of this book, *The Beginning of the End*. I believe the first chapters of Genesis tell us how it is going to be at the end of the world.

People often ask me, When will Jesus return? My response is always the same—we do not know the exact time but God has given us hundreds of prophecies that when fulfilled will tell us that His return is *near*. I believe this time is very near!

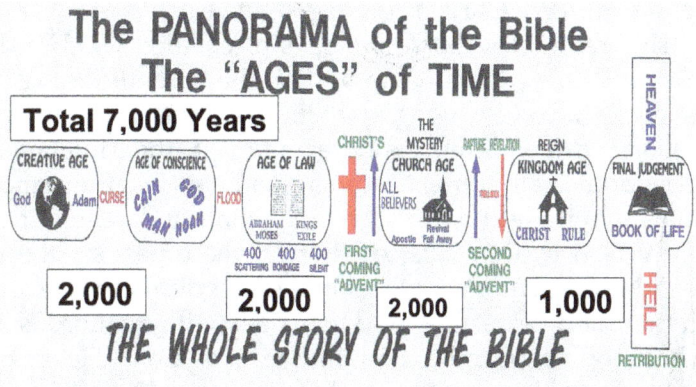

May we review our timeline of history? Someone said *history* is "His Story." Time as we know it has existed for six thousand years with one thousand years yet to come. In these last days, scientists tell us the universe is billions or trillions of years old. How can they say this? They were not there. The definition of science is "to study what can be seen," not to speculate or guess under the guise of science. That would be science fiction. Before recorded history is called prehistoric or prewritten history. Science teaches us today that God did not make the world. It all began with either a big explosion or an alien race who decided to begin our universe. I kid you not!

Here is our time of human existence. From creation to the time of the flood was two thousand years. From the time of the flood to the time of Christ, almost two thousand years, 1,993 years to be exact. The last seven years of Christ's life will be yet to come, the seven-year tribulation period. He was thirty-three years old when He was crucified. Jesus died, was buried, and rose again, and was alive for forty days. He began the church and instituted the church in His thirty-third year. The next time period was from the time Christ instituted the church to His second coming. This period of time will also be two thousand years. The total years from creation to the second coming of Christ is six thousand years.

This resembles the seven days of creation. God said, Seven days you will labor and on the seventh day you shall rest. God is giving mankind six thousand years to labor and then a thousand years to rest (the Millennial Kingdom yet to come). Two thousand plus two thousand plus two thousand adds up to six thousand years. I believe God expected us to labor for these past six thousand years., and then to rest in the Kingdom to come for a thousand years. God said that a day with the Lord is a thousand years and a thousand years as a day. He created the world in six days and God created His world to last six thousand years and during this time we are to labor.

Revival

We live in the time period called the "Church" or the "Times of the Gentiles," which was started when Jesus commissioned His church to *go*:

> Go ye therefore, and teach all nations, baptizing them in the name of the Father, and of the Son, and of the Holy Ghost: Teaching them to observe all things whatsoever I have commanded you: and, lo, I am with you always, even unto the end of the world. – Matthew 28:19–20

Well, that commission has not changed. Jesus instituted the church, knowing it would last two thousand years. We are to "labor" in the fields of the world until He returns. As the end approaches, may we work even more to win this world for Christ.

I believe that the first chapters of Genesis tell us, as Jesus said, "as the days of Noah." How long will this world exist, and are we living in the last days? What do these first chapters in Genesis teach us? First, before Jesus returns mankind will begin to deny the existence of God. Satan began this doubtful thinking in the garden when he said, "Has God said…?" That is exactly what we are teaching in the schools today. Has God said? The answer is yes!

It is time for revival in our land! Great preachers like D.L. Moody, Charles Haddon Spurgeon, and Billy Graham preached all over the world about God's love for His creation. But there are no evangelists today. I thought for sure that Billy Graham was going to see the rapture, but he did not. He lived for 99 years and God sent him home. How many churches do you think are growing? Do not strain your brain—very few, in the United States. We are seeing a great explosion of evangelism around the world. Especially where the antichrist is new to the people. God is harvesting His church around the world.

Maybe, God is giving us a little more time to prepare. Maybe, just maybe, God is holding back His coming so we could be going out and evangelize the world. The day of reaching, missions, and touching people's lives is coming to an end. God is patiently waiting. He is not sitting at the right hand of God but is standing and ready to call His church home. We need to wake up and realize we are living in the very last days, and then the beginning of the New World Order. Look at the news every day and you will see how it lines up with the Book of Genesis.

The fourth Great Event

I believe when we look around the world the number one issue is the destruction of the family. For the first time in human history, more babies are born out of wedlock and to single mothers than babies being born in families with a mother and father. It has become the norm and very acceptable. For six thousand years, being born outside of marriage was looked down upon.

We have many ministries to help single mothers without condemning them but helping them with love and care. But we are not telling them and the rest of the world that this is normal and acceptable. Many unwed mothers must have DNA tests to find out who the father. Stop and think for a moment: if you do not know the father, how many men have you been with?

Children are a precious gift from God. The family was designed by God with a mother and a father working and loving together for their children's welfare. The old Chinese proverb is true: there are no whole eggs in a broken nest.

The theme of this book is to prove that the first part of Genesis tells us how it will be in the last days. We have laid out five Great events that are recorded in Genesis and can be seen in our world today. All of this started in the last 150 years, the "Last Days."

The first major event that tells us Jesus is coming is "Creation." We believe that God created the world. For the first time in human history, we live in a day when scientists and our educational system tell us there is no god and we came about by an explosion or by aliens. Believing and teaching about Creation is vitally important. It is sad that many pastors, schools, and people today are allowing their children to be duped. God help us!

Genesis also teaches us, secondly, that there was a flood. Jesus said as the days of Noah so shall it be when I return. We know the story of Noah is true because we can trace our lineage from three different nations. They migrated after the flood to three parts of the world: Asia, Europe, and Africa.

The third event mentioned was the One World government and one united religion, all being led by one antichrist. Like today, the only religion that was acceptable was the religion of tolerance. Jesus was not tolerant. He said, "I am the way, the truth, and the life: no man cometh unto the Father, but by me" (John 14:6).

The story of the Tower of Babel shows how all religions trace themselves back to Nimrod and the Tower of Babel. All religions are false. Only a relationship with Jesus and being a part of His family can ensure our place in heaven.

On a trip to China in early 2019, my wife and I saw the birthplace of Buddha. The Chinese government spent hundreds of millions of dollars on this beautiful place. They showed how Buddha was birthed out of a lotus plant as a young child of the sun and moon god. There is this huge metal lotus tree, about three stories high, and then it opens up and—behold—there is baby Buddha, about 50 feet high and with his normal potbelly. Most religions can be traced back to the Tower of Babel and Nimrod himself. Any religion that makes man a god or has a mother and son deities is a false religion and had its beginnings in Babel.

Some in the Pentecostal faith today think they have the very power of God and call themselves little gods. We should be empowered by God to do the work of God, but they speak of having the power themselves. Some are called "healing" evangelists. Yes, God heals, but not by our power. That is also heresy.

Sodom and Gomorrah and the Gay Agenda

Now we will look at the fourth Great Event, Sodom and Gomorrah. This chapter will deal with a very sensitive subject: Sodom's sin. When Jesus said, "As the days of Noah were so shall be when the Son of God returns," that's not just the flood, but the things before and after the flood. I believe Sodom's sin ushers in the second coming of Christ. What was Sodom's sin? Homosexuality.

While it is politically incorrect to say that homosexuality is sinful, the Bible calls it an abomination and unnatural. Some of you are saying I should not be judgmental. That may be because you have been snake bitten. You have been duped. Satan has told the world the lie that homosexuality is not only acceptable and should be tolerated but is equal to God's design for man and woman. What I mean as God's design is that—may I be a little crude—the plumbing God gave men and women fit perfectly together and have a God-designed purpose. His purpose from the garden to now is to be fruitful and multiply. Homosexuality does not.

First, let me state my biblical opinion. We should all love homosexuals, but not the sin of homosexuality. We should love thieves, murders, or adulterers, but not the sin of murder, stealing, or adultery. We must look at a person and separate them from their sins. As a pastor, I have led homosexuals to Christ. They know I love them and care for their souls. I am concerned about where they will spend eternity. Remember, we love the sinner, but we do not love their sin. God loves the world but hates our sin.

During my pastoral ministry, I upset many church members by leading homosexuals to Christ and then baptizing them into our church. I was going to baptize a homosexual I led to faith in Christ, and some said, "You cannot baptize that queer in this church." And then I said, "I will baptize him in a lake, but he will be baptized." I told the church leaders, "This fellow came to Christ in our church and we are going to baptize him." We did, and it was in the church. He grew in Christ and abandoned his homosexual lifestyle. I was proud to put my ministry on the line. Remember, the Bible says God so loved the "world" (John 3:16)! That means, everyone—every lifestyle—every color—every nationality—every sinner!

When we speak of Sodom, we are talking about biblical homosexuality. God condemns homosexuality and sodomy. Even the word "sodomy" is unclean and unnatural. God said it was an abomination, not I. There should never be debate or discussion on the merit or sinfulness of sodomy.

Truth today

Here is what is happening in America: we ask ourselves, "Is something right or wrong?" Every society of people needs an absolute authority to determine what is wrong or right. To arrive at an answer, we take a poll, or we ask the "experts." Can I be honest with you? I do not care what Oprah thinks; I do not care what the music industry thinks; I do not care what the movie industry thinks, or anybody on television. Their opinions do not matter to God or to any believer.

Some will say very sternly, "Seventy percent of America is in favor of sodomy." Polls can be manipulated and skewed to favor one side or another. Majorities can be wrong! It does not matter how many agree or disagree. In the days of Noah, a poll was taken and everyone except eight people would not listen to God.

Majorities are not always right. Only God is right one hundred percent of the time. We have lost biblical thinking and teaching. We ask, "Who is right?" Politicians say the majority is always right, except if the majority disagrees with them. Someone said, "How do you know when a politician is lying? When their lips are moving." The only side which is always right is God's side. Moses asked, "Who is on the Lord's side?" (Exodus 32:26). That is how we determine right from wrong.

How about denominations? Can they give us truth? Well, many of the Methodists and Presbyterians are accepting homosexuality as an alternative lifestyle. Well then, they are denying the Word of God. I don't care what any denomination says or believes—I am going the way of the Word of God. It is the Word of God that matters. Who determines what is right and wrong? Not any majority or denomination or even any expert! God and God alone determines what is right or wrong. Amen!

Secondly, who determines what truth is? This is the study of philosophy. I had many philosophy classes and the question that philosophers ask is, "What is truth?" Their answer: "Who's truth? Yours, mine, or someone else's?" Everyone is searching for truth.

We want God's truth. I can tell you what biblical truth is. Jesus said, "I am the way, the truth, and the life" (John 14:6). When we talk about truth, the Word of God is true. Now listen, if the Word of God does not agree with you, guess who is wrong. You are wrong!

As we consider the land of Sodom and the sin of homosexuality, there is only one source of truth. God's Word says that marriage is between a man and a woman. That is how we were created and how we should live. Any other lifestyles are against God and His creation.

Some today say, "That depends." Depends on what? That's what the Bible says. We have questions about divorce, living together, and abortion. Where are the answers? Opinions, polls, or experts? No! The Bible is clear on all the issues. Divorce is allowed but should be after much counseling and prayer. Living together is sinful. That does not mean we hate people who live together, but we must say it is wrong! Some say, "Everybody's doing it." That does not make it right. This also includes issues like gambling or immodest dress. The Bible has clear answers on all important issues. May I add something? Fellows, no one wants to see your underwear. And let me say, ladies, underwear goes under your clothes. That's why they call it underwear.

Homosexuality, which is what Sodom is about. The Bible is clear on this subject. Let's look at just a few verses.

> If a man also lie with mankind, as he lieth with a woman, both of them have committed an abomination: they shall surely be put to death; their blood shall be upon them. – Leviticus 20:13
>
> For this cause God gave them up unto vile affections: for even their women did change the natural use into that which is against nature: And likewise also the men, leaving the natural use of the woman, burned in their lust one toward another; men with men working that which is unseemly, and receiving in themselves that recompence of their error which was meet. And even as they did not like to retain God in their knowledge, God gave them over to a reprobate mind, to do those things which are not convenient. – Romans 1:26–28
>
> Even as Sodom and Gomorrha, and the cities about them in like manner, giving themselves over to fornication, and going after strange flesh, are set forth for an example, suffering the vengeance of eternal fire. – Jude 1:7

> Nevertheless, to avoid fornication, let every man have his own wife, and let every woman have her own husband. – 1 Corinthians 7:2

God performed the first marriage ceremony in the Garden of Eden. God married Adam and Eve. Every time I do a marriage, I quote the same verses used by God in Genesis: "Therefore shall a man leave his father and his mother, and shall cleave unto his wife: and they shall be one flesh" (Genesis 2:24). The Bible says Adam "knew" his wife Eve (Genesis 4:1). We are talking about sex and how God designed it for a man and woman in the holiness of marriage. God created it and He said it is perfect and good within the bonds of marriage.

God created sex for procreation. Look at that word, we are able to pro-"create." We were created in God's image, which means we were given the ability to create life. This is not to be taken lightly or procreate outside of marriage.

Sex is holy—if it were not for sex, none of us would be here. The devil has had sex become dirty. The devil has lured some in the world into unnatural sex. Sex is like dynamite: it is good unless you use it wrongly. Dynamite can open up a landslide in a valley or be used to kill and destroy.

The truth is there are things in this world that God created, and we must obey the rules in order to use it. Sometimes God gives us a gift, but it is to be used by those who are mature enough to respect and understand it. That is why we must be a certain age to be married. You should understand the power of the gift of marriage and procreation.

Here is the truth of the power of procreation between a man and a woman. Each partner shares their 23 chromosomes. The 46 chromosomes unite to make a human being that will live for eighty to a hundred years. That is what I call power! God gives us the permission and the power to create a human being. This miracle is important and beautiful. It should not be made impure by homosexuality, adultery, fornication, or destroyed by abortion. God created it to build families that will love each other and love God who created them. Amen!

Can you believe that we have sanctioned the killing of what God gave us the power to create? God did not give us permission or power to murder and destroy. God help us! Only God gives life and only God can take life.

God married Adam and Eve, not Adam and Steve. God has not changed. Marriage is still between a husband and a wife, and sex in marriage is holy. In ancient Jewish homes, the couple was married in the bride's home and had their marriage night in that home to prove the woman's virginity. Then they went on a long honeymoon so they could get to "know" each other and procreate.

Sodom and Lot's family

In Genesis 13:10, Abraham had given the land east toward Sodom to his adopted son Lot. It was the greenest and best land before it was destroyed. Sodom existed where the Dead Sea is today. Today, everything is dry and dead. Nothing can live there.

What happened to this beautiful garden? Sodom was a sinful and immoral city. Lot was drawn to this city because it was similar to Egypt (Genesis 13:1). He moved in slowly: first, he lived outside the city, then he moved close to the gate, and finally owned a home inside and was assimilated into this sinful city. That is how Satan works, slowly moving us closer to sin until we are dead in sin. Like a moth to a flame, the moth seeks to get as close to the flame and not get burned.

I want you to see this map. My wife and I had been able to make many trips to Israel. Follow the map downwards toward the Dead Sea from the beautiful Galilee area (top of map). This is where you see the body of water

called the Sea of Galilee. This is where most of the miracles were done by Jesus. This is where the Beatitudes were taught, and the feeding of the 5,000 or many more.

Then you travel down the Jordan River. This is where Jesus was baptized. Then you keep going down and it empties into the Dead Sea. Why is it dead? Nothing goes out of it. All the dirt and minerals of the river dump into the Dead Sea and stay there. This is such a good illustration of the results of sin in our lives.

I swam in the Dead Sea—you cannot sink. Everyone floats due to the large amount of salt in the water. You come out of the dead sea and your body is slimy and dirty. Everyone must shower quickly, or you will begin to itch. It is not a pleasant experience.

This is where Sodom and Gomorrah existed. We have gone to the bottom of the Dead Sea and found pottery from Sodom and Gomorrah. God came like an atomic bomb, blew them up with fire, and made a hole so big that the water goes into it and cannot go out. That's what God thinks about sodomy.

Why was Sodom destroyed? Because the penalty, according to Scripture, for the act of homosexuality was to be put to death. You say, "Pastor, why would God do that?" Because He loves us. He knew that the diseases that would come from sodomy (anal sex) would eventually destroy the whole world, before His plan to redeem His creation could be completed by His Son Jesus.

The sexual diseases were spreading so rampantly that the angels sent by God could not find anyone not infected by disease except Lot and his family. If Sodom were allowed to survive, we would not be here today. The diseases that came from sodomy were as deadly as AIDS and syphilis and would have eventually wiped out the human race before it's time.

So, God had to act like a wise physician and cut out the cancer of sodomy. God was trying to heal the world. He is also trying to help all of us today by warning us of the deadly outcomes of homosexual sex.

Behold, this was the iniquity of thy sister Sodom, pride, fulness of bread, and abundance of idleness was in her and in her daughters, neither did she strengthen the hand of the poor and needy. And they were haughty, and committed abomination before me. – Ezekiel 16:49–50

> Then the LORD rained upon Sodom and upon Gomorrah brimstone and fire from the LORD out of heaven; And he overthrew those cities, and all the plain, and all the inhabitants of the cities, and that which grew upon the ground. – Genesis 19:24–25

Sodomy today

We see here that the fourth Great Event from the first part of Genesis is being acted out again in our time and is having the same effect. God said homosexuality is wrong. He does not change. Today, many of the sexual diseases have their origin in homosexuality. Why? Because they are not using the plumbing the way God instructed. The Bible is God's manual to marriage and sex. God created sex, and sex is beautiful, sacred, and holy when we obey His rules in His manual, the Bible! That is why we call it "holy matrimony."

God says to be fruitful, and He has not changed. The Bible states that sex is only allowed between a man and a woman. You cannot have a child any other way. How sad to hear about a child being adopted by a homosexual couple. How confusing it must be. Our children are being forced to read books about Johnny's two dads or Mary's two moms. A homosexual couple cannot be fruitful and multiply because they cannot period! That is how He created mankind and God has not changed.

We do not call homosexuals sodomites anymore. They are now called gay. Changing the name does not change the Word of God. According to God's intolerant Bible, they are sodomites. Today, we are being infected with diseases that come from sodomites.

The people of Sodom said, "We do not have to obey God's rules. We will do it our own way; we call our sin a lifestyle because we think it is acceptable." And what did God do? God came and destroyed them. He used fire to kill all the germs and diseases. Homosexuality and the act of homosexuality is a cancer to our society. God says, "Repent. Change, because your 'lifestyle' can cause death." The Bible says that the wages of sin is death (Romans 6:23).

Can we remember back in the 80s?: the AIDS epidemic, and before that syphilis, and several other venereal diseases. All have their roots in the homosexual community. AIDS is found naturally in apes and chimpanzees, which means sometime in history a homosexual had sex with an ape and it transferred into our human community. Please say, "Yuck."

This is why the Bible says that marriage and sex are between one man and one woman. Why? To keep our marriage and lives pure. Purity is also the only way throughout history to establish the child's mother and father.

Before the flood, when God was looking throughout the whole world for a pure people, He could only find Noah and his wife and their children. The world was so infected with diseases, and society was so sick, that God sent a flood to purify it.

See, Sodom had a similar problem in Genesis 19. Sin and disease were so rampant that God had to purify Sodom if the world was to continue to exist. Like a skilled surgeon, God chose to purify the world by destroying Sodom. The Lord rained down on Sodom and Gomorrah brimstone and fire. Why fire? Fire is purifying. Everything in Sodom was infected and polluted and needed to be cleansed. The land, houses, and people were all infected. It had to be completely destroyed. This is why there is a very deep hole we call the Dead Sea. God gave humanity a second, or if we include the flood, a third chance to continue to exist.

The Bible uses the word abomination to define the homosexual lifestyle. Here is what the Bible says:

> Thou shalt not lie with mankind, as with womankind: it is abomination. – Leviticus 18:22
>
> If a man also lie with mankind, as he lieth with a woman, both of them have committed an abomination: they shall surely be put to death; their blood shall be upon them. – Leviticus 20:13
>
> For this cause God gave them up unto vile affections: for even their women did change the natural use into that which is against nature: And likewise also the men, leaving the natural use of the woman, burned in their lust one toward another; men with men working that which is unseemly, and receiving in themselves that recompence of their error which was meet. And even as they did not like to retain God in their knowledge, God gave them over to a reprobate mind, to do those things which are not convenient. – Romans 1:26–28

Both Jesus and both Old and New Testaments approve only sexual relationships between a husband and wife. This is the historical teaching of both Judaism and Christianity. We do not have the freedom to change this because our society has changed. God has not changed.

As a pastor, when I have ministered to the homosexual community, I found many of them are alcoholics, deeply depressed, and even suicidal. Some say this is because of the way we treat them. No! It is because, in their minds, they feel dirty, they feel wrong and sinful. The only solution is the precious blood of the Lord Jesus that cleanses them from sin.

Americans radically overestimate the LGBT population. Some polls and news agencies want us to believe it is 10 percent—some even say 25 percent—of the population. That is one-quarter of the population. Here are the real results: Gallup's more accurate poll, which was done in 2017, estimates that 4.5 percent of Americans are LGBT, based on respondents' self-identification as being lesbian, gay, bisexual, or transgender. We have over 350 million Americans.

We as a society are swallowing all the lies of the homosexual agenda. Look at the music, movies, and television today, from Ellen DeGeneres and Disney shows to movies like *Brokeback Mountain*. Homosexuality is being elevated to an unhealthy level. The entertainment industry is giving a platform to the LGBT community. Today, they flood our society with their agendas. New cartoons and children's books are coming out that display homosexuality as a normal lifestyle and not to be criticized. Their agenda is to make the LGBT lifestyle normal and acceptable.

It is working and it is also affecting the Christian community, especially young people. It is rampant in our society and all who criticize this agenda are immediately fired. Many television preachers will not take a stand against homosexuals. They are afraid of being taken off the television and losing their financial support. If a news reporter or paper ever printed something negative about homosexuality, they would be immediately fired.

It started with a television show called *Soap*, where Billy Crystal played an openly homosexual man; later, a television sitcom called *Will and Grace*; and now talk show host Ellen DeGeneres. Slowly, they are gaining exposure in our society. The Devil has a plan and is very patient. He is doing exactly what he did in Sodom: making man a god and telling mankind to disobey God's Word.

In many liberal churches, they are preaching about loving one another even those who defy God's Word. Homosexuals have their own churches—the Metropolitan Community Church. Here's what they believe: Jesus was a homosexual. This is what they think is true. They say that Jesus and John were a homosexual couple. They also believe that King David was a homosexual. They say David and Jonathan were a couple. That is what they preach and believe. All of their sermon themes are the same: God is love, judge not, and be kind to your neighbor. There is nothing wrong with those sermons. But we are instructed to preach the whole Bible, not only the politically correct verses. We must proclaim the authority of the Word of God.

Under President Obama, our White House was adorned with rainbow lights. Later, the same was done for the empire state building. Both were to celebrate the LGBT community. In our schools, our children are being taught that the Bible cannot be trusted. They are also taught that homosexuals are a minority group. They are told that anyone who speaks against them is a bigot or a homophobe. They are being indoctrinated daily by this teaching. Our children and society are being duped, and worst of all we allow them to teach this heresy.

Homosexuals have always been around but in the closet. They have exited the closet these past 150 years. Homosexuality is being lifted up as an elite group in our world. They are wanting to be portrayed as not only equal but superior to other people.

Here is what the Bible says in 1 John 2:15-17:

> Love not the world, neither the things that are in the world. If any man love the world, the love of the Father is not in him. For all that is in the world, the lust of the flesh, and the lust of the eyes, and the pride of life, is not of the Father, but is of the world. And the world passeth away, and the lust thereof: but he that doeth the will of God abideth for ever.

The Bible says the world is filled with liars because the Prince of this World, Satan, is the prince of liars. Many people say, "I disagree with their lifestyle, but I would rather just ignore the issue." But there is a mindset or philosophy that goes with this homosexual lifestyle and it has and will destroy our society.

How does this lifestyle affect us? The homosexual lifestyle is defying God and His Word. They are luring innocent children into this lust-filled lifestyle. We are allowing homosexuals to adopt children and raise them in a sinful environment. Many homosexuals were sexually abused as children, and because of this abuse, they repeat this abuse on other children. If they were sexually abused by the opposite sex, they are turned off from natural sex and are lured into homosexuality. That is why we need to have sympathy and love them in Jesus' name, and at the same time make them realize that homosexuality is not acceptable to God.

Let us approach this issue scientifically. Many in society say they are born that way. This opinion has never been proven. What has been studied and shown to be true is that some traumatic experience had shaken the child's sexual development. We also see that when a child is reaching puberty, they sometimes question their sexuality. If they are taught in school to experiment in alternate sexualities, they made be lured away in guilt to a sinful lifestyle. Many of these children have not even gotten to a point where they understand what is right and wrong. The sad part of all this is that the schools are reinforcing the child to experiment in alternate lifestyles.

Conclusion

Here are three truths from God's Word. Number one, homosexuality can be cured. I can tell you, friends, there are thousands of ex-homosexuals that are coming to know Christ and having families and having children and being changed in Jesus' name. Amen

Secondly, homosexuals are to be loved. We are never to look down on them. Friends, but by the grace of God it could be you. What's the difference between a drug addict and a homosexual? Nothing. All sin is sin. When I was working with the military back in my college days, a homosexual man came into our center. I shared the plan of salvation with him, he wept, and I led him to Christ. He came to the Bible studies. He was excited about becoming a Christian. Then he disappeared. He came back about a month later, weeping and crying. I said, "What happened?" He said, "I fell back in my sinful lifestyle. Please help me." You know what I did? I hugged him. I prayed with him and I said, "Get back in there. We can do all things through Christ!"

Number three, homosexuality is antisocial, antiscriptural, and antisalvation. You cannot come to know Christ without repenting of this sin. This is what the Bible says: you must come to Christ and confess your sins to become a born again Christian.

This is what alcoholics believe. First, admit you have a problem. God still loves you. You can fail, but you have to repent before you can change. This is the best truth: Jesus loves all people, even while we are sinners. He loves us, warts and all. He loves us unconditionally. Here's what the Bible says, "For God so loved the world, that he gave his only begotten son" (John 3:16). He loves homosexuals, but He does not love their sin.

> Know ye not that the unrighteous shall not inherit the kingdom of God? Be not deceived: neither fornicators, nor idolaters, nor adulterers, nor effeminate, nor abusers of themselves with mankind, Nor thieves, nor covetous, nor drunkards, nor revilers, nor extortioners, shall inherit the kingdom of God. And such were some of you. – 1 Corinthians 6:9–11

Paul was saying, "Do not forget you were just like them; you are no better." We are all sinners needing God's forgiveness and grace. I will tell you this: look at that list—you are probably guilty of some of those sins. You are no better. But good news! God loves us just the way we are. The Bible says, "While we were yet sinners, Christ died for us" (Romans 5:8).

This is the message of the Gospel. God loves us just as we are and will change us into new creatures and become like Christ! The message of the Gospel is not hate. It is love through Jesus Christ.

My message and the purpose of this book is to inform as many churches and as many people of the truth of the second coming of Christ. Do not be duped or swayed by the devil. We are living in the days of Sodom and Gomorrah once again. We need to stand up for what is right and do what is truth.

Here is what we learned from the story of Sodom:
Stay away from sin or you will be burned.
We are living in the day of Sodom once again.
We must prepare for Christ's second coming!

Abraham did not have children and God told him, "Your offspring will be like the stars in the sky, like the sands of the deserts." He answered, "Huh, I don't have any offspring." So he adopted his nephew Lot and he said to Lot, "You are my son, you are my firstborn." He gave Lot half of his inheritance and Lot said, "Give me the part toward Sodom." The closer he got to Sodom, the more sinful he became.

Every one of us tries to get as close to sin as we can. My wife babysits our twin grandchildren. I built a little gate in the playroom. They have got tens and tens of toys in the playroom. But they want to get out of the gate. Why? Because they always want what they cannot have.

You and I are the same way. Do not criticize Adam and Eve, my friends. You would be biting into an apple tomorrow if it was up to you. All of us try to get as close as we can to sin.

The story is not over. After Lot leaves Sodom, he takes his sinful habits and two daughters with him. He gets drunk and has intercourse with his daughters. They give birth to the Moabites and the Ammonites, who became the enemies of the Jews throughout history.

What have we learned? Sin has a consequence. My word to you today, my friends, is that this is not just about homosexuality. Some of you are getting very close to sin and you are going to get burned. Stay away. Stay in church, keep your kids in church. Keep your kids in the Word. Teach them the truth. Because in these last days, we need to make sure we got everybody on board the "Ark," because the flood is coming. Let's stand together.

FIFTH GREAT EVENT

The Patriarchs – Sons of Abraham at War

This chapter is the last, but it is the most important. Some people ask, "How do we know the Bible is the Word of God?" "Keep your eye on the State and people of Israel. God has and will work miracles with His people." The State of Israel can also show us when Jesus will return. Again, keep your eye on the State and people of Israel. God has never forgotten His people. He will return for His chosen people. The Patriarchs is the fifth and last Great Event, which I believe will usher in the second coming of Jesus Christ. For four thousand years, Jews and Arabs have been a major part of our world. Why is the Middle East so important? The Middle East, and especially Israel, are at the crossroads between China, Europe, and Africa.

Review

Let us review our timeline: from the time of creation to the time of the flood was two thousand years. How do you know that? Because the Bible gives us the genealogies of the people who lived. It's not rocket science. Second, from the time of the flood to Christ's death was also two thousand years. Lastly, from the time of

Christ's resurrection to our days today it has been nearly two thousand years. He told His disciples, "I will come again!" Jesus instituted the church in the year 33. So two thousand years from that time will be 2033, which is right around the corner. I am not saying that 2033 is the date, but what I am telling you is that it is close to that date. We must be ready!

Turn to Genesis 11—right after the flood, the sons of Noah divided into three separate tribes: Japheth went to Europe, Ham went to Africa, and Shem went to Asia and the Middle East. Shem received the blessing of God and from his tribe came Abraham and his descendants.

God said in His Word that a day with the Lord is a thousand years and a thousand years is as a day (2 Peter 3:8). I believe the six days of creation are a clue to Jesus' return. God said, "Six days you labor," and on the seventh day, He rested. God's creation has lasted six thousand years and we have labored for these past six thousand years. There is a seventh millennium coming. A thousand-year Millennial Kingdom has been promised and will be established soon. During this time, we will live and reign with Christ in His promised Kingdom.

Prior to the Kingdom, God will send a seven-year period of tribulation to the world. He will judge this world for its sin and rebellion. Remember, Jesus was crucified (cut off) at thirty-three years of age. Seven years before He would have established His Kingdom at the age of forty. Now God will start the clock again and finish His work of Judgment before He establishes His Kingdom.

Let us review our teaching. I believe the first chapters of Genesis tell us when Jesus is coming again. There are five Great Events in Genesis that have occurred again in the last 150 years, to show when He will return.

Number one, God's creation. For the first time in history, mankind has denied the existence and creation of God. 150 years ago, Darwin wrote about evolution and man accepted it as fact. For six thousand years, nobody denied creation. It has only been in the last 150 years that man has denied, foolishly, the existence of God. Evolution and the philosophy that comes from evolution has brought us Communism, Nazism, Abortion, and Racism. Today, evolution is more than a scientific theory; it has changed our lives and society forever.

The number two Great Event which we see occurring again in our world today, is Noah and the flood. The Bible says as the days of Noah, so shall it be when Jesus shall return. How were the days of Noah? They were filled with corruption, murder, disease, abortion, death.

How was it? There was a population explosion. We are in the same situation today. Our planet is running out of food, water, and air. We are maxed out. Think for a moment: our planet earth is like a spaceship. We are traveling at one thousand miles an hour around the sun, and we are spinning on its axis at one thousand miles per hour. As we go through the universe, we only have so much water, food, and air. We cannot go anywhere else and get more of it. God says, I have set an alarm for my creation, when you run out or destroy all your resources I will return!

How was it? There was great moral corruption. I remember showing a movie at my church called *The Clock*

Watchers. It is about a Bible teacher who travels from 150 years ago to our present time. He goes to the mall to a movie and is shocked at the immorality. What shocks him most is that it does not shock any of the Christians he meets.

The third Great Event was the Tower of Babel. How was it? There was an increase in arts and industry. The Bible said that Nimrod built this Tower in Babel. Nimrod begins astrology, and the religious worship of mother and son gods named Baal and Ashtaroth. Today we see the new age movement and the religion of tolerance.

How was it? The whole world was united as one. They had one language, one religion, and followed one leader. In the last days, man will want, a One World government, One World economy, One World religion, and all wearing the Mark of the Beast.

The Fourth Great event was the destruction of Sodom. There was a diseased land called Sodom, which God destroyed for our safety. We get the act of sodomy from the wicked nation. We do not like to speak about this subject, but we are living in a day and an hour where people think this lifestyle is acceptable.

We are called to be salt and light in this sin-cursed world. But we have lost our light and have become lukewarm in our influence. Do you know what the problem in the world is today? Many say this world is falling apart. The problem is not the world. The problem is the church. The church is doing exactly what the world is doing! We have lost our influence. The church has lost its salt. The church has lost its light.

If we turned all the lights out, you would stumble into the church pews, all of us trying to find a way out. If I took a small light, all the eyes would be upon me and I could say, "Follow me. I know where the exits are. Follow me." This is what a Christian is supposed to be like.

Somebody needs to stand up, somebody needs to speak out, somebody needs to take a stand. We are all compromising. And the world goes to hell without Jesus.

The fifth Great Event

The fifth and last Great Event we see in Genesis that are seen today and point to the second coming of Christ is the Patriarchs. We begin with Abraham, who lived near Babel in a town named Ur. Chapter 11 begins with the Tower of Babel and the dispersion of the people and the confusion of the tongues. Abraham and his wife Sarah were without children. Abraham was wealthy for a man of his time.

Abraham's descendants were given a promise of great blessings. Here is the problem: Abraham had no descendants. This fifth Great Event is the war between Abraham's descendants, throughout all of these four thousand years.

God's promise to Abraham was to be given to Abraham's firstborn son. Here is the problem: there were four descendants who claim the land, seed, and promise. The firstborn descendants are Lot, Ismael, Isaac, and grandson Esau. All of the past crusades and Middle East wars with all the terrorism can be traced back to this firstborn fiasco. Abraham did not trust God enough to provide a miracle birth of a son and heir. He tried to provide himself an heir by adoption and adultery. Neither had good results.

The last of the Great Events in Genesis that shows us when Jesus will return is the descents of Abraham. The Jewish people were given the land of Israel because they are the true descendants of Abraham. They lost their land when they disobeyed God and left the land to go to Egypt until the Exodus. They fought to get their land back under General Joshua. Their kingdom was expanded under King David. They were conquered and dispersed by

Babylon and Assyria. But all the prophets promised they would return to their land in the last days. Why are we seeing ancient biblical lands spotlighted today? Because where the world began is where the world ends!

Abraham and his brothers took for themselves wives. His brothers had children, but not Abraham and his wife. Now, Abraham's father Terah told Abraham to take his nephew Lot as his son. He accepted Lot as his son, which was the law at this time.

> Now the Lord had said unto Abram, Get thee out of thy country, and from thy kindred, and from thy father's house, unto a land that I will shew thee: And I will make of thee a great nation, and I will bless thee, and make thy name great; and thou shalt be a blessing: And I will bless them that bless thee, and curse him that curseth thee: and in thee shall all families of the earth be blessed. So Abram departed, as the Lord had spoken unto him; and Lot went with him: and Abram was seventy and five years old when he departed out of Haran. And Abram took Sarai his wife, and Lot his brother's son, and all their substance that they had gathered, and the souls that they had gotten in Haran; and they went forth to go into the land of Canaan; and into the land of Canaan they came. – Genesis 12:1–5

Abraham was visited by two angels who said to him, "Stop trying and start trusting! You are going to have a baby with Sarah." He said, "Listen, my lords, those days are gone—my wife and I are too old." Well, Sarah conceived and bore a son. Abraham named the child "laughter" because Sarah laughed and said, this would never happen. Nothing is impossible with God!

They also prophesied that, in the last days, Babylon and Assyria will once again be in the news. You may say,

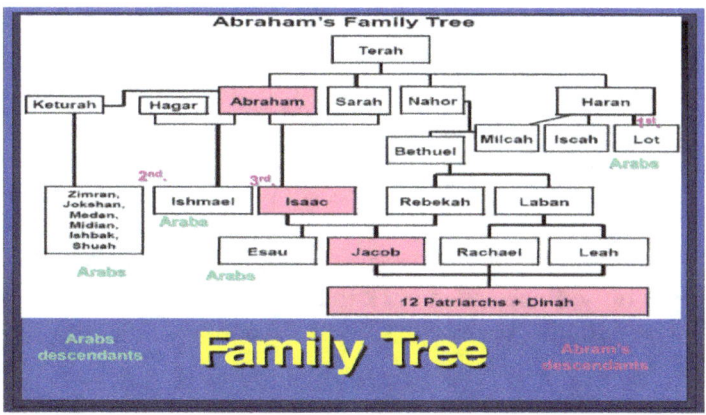

"No, they are not." Yes, they are! Iraq, Iran, and Syria are those ancient lands today.

In Genesis 12, Abraham and his family were told, right after the flood, to get out of the land of his fathers and follow God's leadership to a new Promised Land, later called Israel. Abraham obeyed God and left the land of "moon worship" and went to the Promised Land. "Get out of that land." We should remember this and keep from all false religions.

In Genesis 11, the Bible tells us of Abraham who lived in the city of Ur which was near Babel. Most of the people in this area worshiped the moon goddess Ashtaroth. Abraham believed in God and rejected moon worship. God was pleased with Abraham and spoke to him and said, "Get out of this land." God led Abraham and his family to the Promised Land, modern-day Israel.

Have you ever noticed an Arab nation's flag? They all have a crescent moon somewhere on the flag. This moon worship theology dates to the time after the flood. God said to Abraham, "Get out of that land and go to a land where I will prosper you." He obeyed God and God gave him the land of Israel.

The Muslim faith has its roots in moon worship. Muhammad incorporated moon worship into Islamic beliefs because all the Arabs already worshipped the moon. Mecca and Medina were both steeped in moon worship. So was Ur, where Abraham lived. Mecca and Medina were holy places even back then.

The Muslim word for God is "Allah" which was the name of a moon god in Babel. In fact, "Allah" is the personal name of the moon god, the chief among the three-hundred sixty pagan idols that were worshipped in Mecca, the hometown of Muhammad. The Muslim "holy" month of Ramadan starts at the sighting of a new crescent moon. Muslims pray bowing toward the Kaaba (the big rock) in Mecca five times a day. This big black rock was an idol to the moon god of Mecca.

Many of you might have seen a big black rock in Mecca, Saudi Arabia. They believe it fell down from the moon. They call it the devil's rock. They go to Mecca on a pilgrimage called a *hajj*. When they get to the rock, they walk around the rock and throw rocks at the rock (silly, I know).

The big "Black Stone," or Kaaba Stone, is a Muslim relic. The stone is a black rock, polished smooth by the hands of millions of pilgrims. Most non-Muslims believe it to be a meteorite. Muslims around the world face Mecca five times a day and pray to this piece of "moon rock."

Why do they worship at a place dedicated to a rock? Babylon was a city of moon worshippers. Throughout Jewish history, what did the Jews continue to do? They kept worshiping Baal and Ashtoreth. God sent prophets to call Israel to repent and forsake false gods. The Jewish people, like most people in the olden times, were agricultural communities. They heard of these false gods who would send rain and good weather, so they offered sacrifices to these false gods. So sad! We would not do that, would we?

Most of our holidays (holy days) come from these false gods. I am not against celebrating Christmas or Easter or any holiday. But we should know it's history and steer clear of any false worship.

Different names, same false god. She is mentioned in the Hebrew Bible as Ashtoreth, the wife of Baal. So, Baal is the masculine god and Ashtoreth is the female goddess. Baal is a celebration of the sun-god and Ashtoreth is a celebration of the moon-god.

Why do we celebrate these two deities? After the Catholic Church evangelized a new country, they thought it was wise to incorporate their pagan beliefs into Catholic beliefs. This was done over and over again. The old pagan beliefs were gone, but not completely. It is too late to change these holidays—they are a part of our daily lives. But always remember that all false religions go back to the Tower of Babel.

The Jews continued to worship false gods throughout their history. Even when Moses was up on the mount to receive the Ten Commandments, he came down and the Jews were dancing naked around a statue of Baal, asking for fertility in their land. They were asking mother-god, Ashtaroth, to have sex with her child-husband, Baal, the sun-god. If the sex was fruitful, there would be plenty of crops. Unfortunately, the foolish Jews fell for that every time.

God made Abraham's name great and his descendants a blessing to the world. The second part of God's promise is also true: God has blessed any nation that has blessed Israel, and God has cursed any nation who has cursed Israel.

The Old Testament records the many events of Abraham's descendants. The Koran also records a false—but still interesting—history of Abraham's descendants.

There have been many battles that were fought by Israel to regain the land. God miraculously won the battles for Israel even when Israel was outnumbered. God has shown His power and presence in the mighty miracles we find in the Old Testaments. The Bible tells us how God sent down fire when Elijah challenged the worship of Baal and idolatry. God is not finished with the people and descendants of Abraham. He is still working miracles in the life of His chosen people.

Let us look at the history and importance of the descendants of Abraham. We believe that there are three patriarchs: Abraham, Isaac, and Jacob. Abraham was given a promise that his descendants would be like the sands of the sea and God would bless those that bless his children. But here is the problem: Abraham did not trust God.

Abraham decides to adopt his nephew Lot, and by adopting Lot he gives Lot half of his kingdom. Lot wants the land toward Sodom, and we saw how sinful Sodom was in the last chapter. Sodom is destroyed by fire because of their sinfulness. Lot escapes Sodom's destruction with his two daughters. He becomes drunk and commits incest with his two daughters. (Yuk!) They are both impregnated with Abraham's seed. They have two sons who grow up to be another enemy and firstborn descendant of Abraham (Moabites and Ammonites). Abraham decides Lot was not the promised descendant.

> Thus were both the daughters of Lot with child by their father. And the first born bare a son, and called his name Moab: the same is the father of the Moabites unto this day. And the younger, she

> also bare a son, and called his name Benammi: the same is the father of the children of Ammon unto this day. – Genesis 19:36–38

Abraham decides once again to do it himself without God's help. He has relations with Hagar, his wife's handmaiden. Hagar has a son named Ishmael. Ishmael grows and at age 12, God tells Abraham that Ishmael is not the promised descendant. God said to Abraham, "I will give you a miraculous child in your old age." By the way, 12 years old is when a Jew becomes a man during bar mitzvah. Ismael is cast away because of Sarah's jealousy. But because of the promise given to Abraham's descendants, Ismael is rescued and prospers and has 12 sons who become the princes of the Arab nations. They all believe they are the promised descendants and Abraham's firstborn sons.

Abraham has another child with a woman named Keturah. One modern commentator on the Hebrew Bible has called Keturah "the most ignored significant person in the Bible."[11] Keturah bore six sons to Abraham, who also believe they are the true descendants of Abraham. Keturah says, "My children deserve the kingdom." The reason we are battling once again in Israel today is that all of those firstborns want their inheritance. But the Bible says it belongs to the Jews.

Isaac had twin boys, Esau and Jacob. Esau was the firstborn but sold his birthright for a bowl of beans. (So many people sell their soul for less.) Esau hated his brother Jacob for betraying him and stealing the birthright. The Book of Genesis refers to the descendants of Jacob's brother Esau as the Edomites. Today, the people of Jordan are considered descendants of the Edomites. They also think the land of Israel belongs to them. What a mess!

Today, all eyes are on Iraq, Iran, and Syria. Why? Because this is where the Garden of Eden existed. This is where the Ark landed. This is where the Tower of Babel was built. This is where the children of Israel were taken captive because they worshipped Baal and Ashtaroth. This is where Daniel lived and prophesied the rebuilding of the Temple. This is where Nehemiah and Ezra left from, to rebuild the walls and Temple. This is why this area of the Middle East is on the news nightly. God says the area where civilization began is where civilization will end.

As we close this book, let's review our timeline: from the time of creation to the time of the flood was two thousand years; from the time of the flood to the death of Jesus Christ was 1,993 years (seven years short of the two thousand years). From the ascension to the rapture is two thousand years. This time period will end with the rapture of the church. This is when Jesus comes and calls His church home.

The Bible says then shall come seven years of great tribulation. Jesus then returns as King of Kings and Lord of

Lords and battles the forces of evil. He is victorious and recreates the universe, then all of the believers will live and reign with King Jesus for a thousand years. Amen! Amen! Praise the Lord!

Where are we? I believe we are at the cusp of the last six thousand years. I also believe the first 12 chapters of Genesis tell us how it will be at the end of these six thousand years. The world began in the Middle East of Iraq, Iran, and Syria. This is where it will end. This is why these nations are on the news nightly. Jesus is coming!

Rebuilding the Temple

I am reminded of Elijah who called down fire from heaven and consumed all the false gods and called the people of God to repent. God hated it when His people followed these false gods. He felt they had committed adultery with the world. Everything the Jews did, all the feast days, all the sacrifices, everything was done in order to prepare for the Messiah (Jesus).

Jesus was born in the fullness of time. Now, one thing had to be done before the Messiah would come. They had to have a Temple. You cannot have a real Messiah without the Temple. Jesus was dedicated at the Temple. Jesus was in the Temple as a young child and astonished the priests and rabbis. He went into the Temple and turned the money tables over. He went into the Temple and said, "Today, this prophecy has been fulfilled." You had to have a Temple for the Messiah.

In 2019, President Trump came into Jerusalem and recognized Israel as the owner of Jerusalem and he promised to help them build a Temple. The people of Israel were so happy they made a new coin. You see another figure behind Trump? That was Cyrus. Cyrus was the one who allowed the Jews to go back and build the Temple. The people of Israel are calling Trump the new Cyrus. He is allowing us to build the Temple.

In 2020, President Trump made a peace agreement with Israel and some of their neighbors. This is one more peace plan we have seen in these last days. The media has ignored this because they do not like Trump. But it all works together in God's last days plan.

The only prophesy keeping Jesus from coming is the rebuilding of the Temple. I have been on the Temple Mount. There is a mosque there, but the mosque is not built where the Ark of the Covenant and the Temple stood. If you look in the pictures of the Temple Mount, there is a big platform, probably the size of a football field, next to the dome of the rock. That is where the Temple existed and can be rebuilt.

It may not be a Jewish Temple at first, but a Temple of Tolerance to all religions. Who knows? When Moses and Elijah come, they will take ownership of the Temple and they will consecrate the Temple to the Messiah. The two witnesses will be killed by the antichrist and their bodies will be shown to the world. After three and a half years, the Temple is dedicated to the antichrist. The antichrist sets up his image in the Temple, and receives worship and praise, then the Bible says will come "sudden destruction" (1 Thessalonians 5:3). Everything's ready.

There are some people in Israel called the "Temple Faithful." They have collected all the Temple furniture. I had the privilege to see some of the collection on one of my trips to Israel. I am told they have the Ark of the Covenant, Menorah candle, the Table of Showbread, and all the other furniture designed by God and given to Moses. They are breeding red heifers (thought to be a lost breed), once used in sacrifice in the Temple.

If Jesus is to return, there must be a Temple. There had to be a Temple when Jesus first came.

> And there was given me a reed like unto a rod: and the angel stood, saying, Rise, and *measure the Temple of God*, and the altar, and them that worship therein. But the *court which is without the temple* leave out, and measure it not; for it is given unto the Gentiles: and the holy city shall they tread under foot forty and two months. – Revelation 11:1–2

Revelation also tells us that two witnesses for God will appear and announce the second coming of Jesus. Revelation 11:3 says, "And I will give power unto my two witnesses, and they shall prophesy a thousand two hundred and threescore days, clothed in sackcloth." They are described as Moses and Elijah, who come down into the Temple and measure it. This was God taking ownership of the Temple.

I believe Moses and Elijah have the job of announcing the major events of Messiah Jesus. They are first seen, on that Mount of Transfiguration. They were announcing that Jesus was starting His ministry. They are seen again, after the crucifixion when Jesus was placed in the tomb. The Bible says *two men* stood by the tomb. Not two angels. These two men, I believe were Moses and Elijah announcing the resurrection. Then we look at the ascension. Jesus was caught up in the ascension and the two men said, "This same Jesus, which is taken up from you into heaven, shall so come in like manner as ye have seen him go into heaven" (Acts 1:11). He went away on a cloud and He will return on the clouds.

When the Temple is rebuilt, these two men will announce Jesus' second coming. I believe they are Moses and Elijah; it says one called down fire from heaven and the other brought the plagues to Egypt. We know who they are. They will usher in the second coming of Christ.

Problems in the Middle East

We must realize that we are living in biblical times today. I want you to keep your eyes on Israel. All the Middle East problems arise because of the four firstborn sons of Abraham. They have been battling ever since Genesis. There is nothing new under the sun. Everything we see happening has been laid out. It is only a fool that would not look and say, "Oh my goodness, this is exactly what the Bible says will happen!"

Here are Abraham's descendants. First of all, there is Lot and Lot has two descendants who became the enemies of Israel. Then there is Ishmael, who has 12 sons, who are also the enemies of Israel. Then there is Esau, who was the firstborn twin. Isaac has two sons: Esau and Jacob. Esau was deceived and sold his birthright for a bowl of beans. Then we know that Keturah had six sons. Each one of these descendants thinks they own the land of Israel. What a mess!

In the last 150 years, the Arabs met together and said, "Let us rewrite history. We want the land. We want the place of our father Abraham. We want it now! If we cannot have it, we will destroy it for the Jews."

Well, we know who was given the land and also given the promise. It was Jacob, who wrestled with an angel and in that wrestling, God said, "You are my chosen son. I am changing your name from Jacob, meaning 'schemer,' to Israel, which means 'to contend, to fight.'" Jacob and his descendants have been fighting ever since he was given the land.

The new nation of Israel, which started in 1948, is the number one reason for the second coming of Christ. I was born in 1952—this occurred four years before I was born. Israel became a nation. That told us that Jesus is coming soon! The Bible says the generation that sees Israel back in their land will see the second coming of Jesus.

It has been two thousand years since the time of Christ's first advent. The Jews lost their land because of idolatry and disobedience. But now, the Jews are back in the land. For over 2,500 years Israel has been ruled by every nation small and great. But *now*! Israel has returned and is preparing for the coming second advent of Jesus. The Bible is alive. Once again, we are living in biblical times. It was written and *now* fulfilled!

Unfortunately, the church of Jesus Christ is sleeping. Many churches today are dying or barely hanging on. How sad! Today, there is a great erosion of the faith. The Bible said in the last days, the church will be called the Laodicean Church. This church is called "Lukewarm" church. It is time to wake up and get ready!

The Jews have had a four thousand-year history. They know exactly who they are and where they came from. Many years ago, I heard a Rabbi speak. This Rabbi had studied the genealogies of the Jewish people. He could trace your lineage and tell you the tribe your family came from. He said the name Myers is of the tribe of Levi, the priestly tribe. He told the crowd, "We Jews should be waiting and preparing for the Messiah." He did not believe in Jesus. But he was half right: the Messiah Jesus is coming! So, they are just waiting and will be surprised when they see Jesus!

Why is Israel so important? The Bible says, "This is your land and I will give it to you, Israel." The Bible said, "Do not leave the land!" The promise given to Jacob included him staying in the land. He disobeyed and went to Egypt. They went down for four hundred years of bondage. Moses came and delivered them, but they had to fight their way back into the land of Israel.

Who do they have to fight? The 12 sons of Ishmael. Who do they have to fight? The sons of Esau. Who do they have to fight? The sons of the Lot. They had to fight their way back into the land and God said, "Now that you are finally back in, follow my commandments."

They fought their way back into Israel. They continued disobedience and worship false gods. Because they disobeyed, they were divided and conquered. Who conquered Israel? The other sons of Abraham, Iraq and Iran—the Assyrians and the Babylonians. Why? Because the Bible says those two nations are going to be the enemies of Israel. We are seeing these two nations today come to be important, and they are very vocal about their hatred of Israel.

Then the Bible says the Jews will return to the land of Israel from every corner of the earth. God said, "When you see Israel returning to their land, I am coming back." Israel had drifted into idolatry and God took away their land and scattered the Jewish people around the world. For two thousand years, they have been waiting, then World War II and the Holocaust. Because of the Holocaust, Israel was given back their land, and from that time on we have been living in biblical times. Jesus is coming soon!

Conclusion

How long can that generation last? I do not know. The Bible uses the term "generation" with many different amounts of years. I always thought Jesus would come before Billy Graham died. Billy Graham was the last of the great evangelists. Where are the evangelistic preachers today?

Remember what I said about 150 years. When you hear people talk about prophecy, they want to talk about our recent events. Especially, since the time of the sixties when people turned on, like me, and dropped out and made a mess of their lives. That is not the last days.

The last days had been the last 150 years. That is when evolution started. That is when the Industrial Revolution started. In the last 150 years, we began to travel by automobiles, planes and now we have rocket ships. Why? Because the Bible says in the last days there will be an increase in speed and education. More people have a college education today than all the people who had a higher education throughout history.

A hundred fifty years ago, a new movement began, called Zionism. The First Zionist Conference was held in 1897. It was headed by Theodor Benyamin Ze'ev Herzl. He said, "We want to be back in our land, the land of Israel."

In 1897, the Zionists went to Israel and started farming communities. Many of them died, but they never surrendered. I remember that on one of my trips to Israel, a tour guide named Jack knew more about Jesus than most of the theologians. But he was an unbeliever. I witnessed to him at the Garden of Gethsemane. We laid on the grass, right where Jesus knelt in the garden. I asked him, "Do you believe Jesus was the Messiah of Israel?" He grabbed some of the earth right from the base of the olive tree and squeezed out the dirt from between his fingers and said, "This is my Messiah. This earth is my Messiah, my country Israel." Many of the Jews today do not believe in God. As strange as it may seem, many of the Jews are atheists. My friend Jack was an atheist.

He said, "This land was promised to my father, and I will never give it away." That, my friend, is Zionism.

Islamic fundamentalists began 150 years ago. Shiite Muslims are the destructive branch of Islam; they are the killers, they are the terrorists. Their goal is the complete destruction of Israel. They deny the Holocaust and even the heritage and history of Israel. They also bomb Sunni Muslims. Sunni and Shiite Muslims are the two sects of the Islamic faith. They both decided to fight Zionism vocally and militarily. They are furious that Israel exists and want to destroy every Jewish person. We are living in a day when the sons of Abraham are fighting again.

Where are we? We are living in biblical times. Iraq, Iran, and Syria are where the Garden of Eden and the Ark existed.

One last look at Israel. The Bible says the deserts of Israel will bloom in the last days. Today, Israel's number one export is fruit and vegetables. The Bible says peace will come to Israel. But before Jesus returns, many will say, "Peace, peace," but there will be no peace. Every time there is a vote that concerns Israel in the United Nations, most of the nation's vote against Israel. Why? Because the Bible said the world will be against them. When you see the three nations (Iran, Iraq, and Syria) fighting the Jewish people, the return of Jesus is soon. When you see Israel back in their land, Jesus is coming again!

You did not read about this in the news. This man is Jerusalem's Rabbi Yitzhak Kaduri. He died in 2006. He was

the holiest man in Judaism. Every Jew knows and respects him. He had a vision. He wrote his vision down and he gave it to his successor. He said, "Do not read this letter until I am dead." This is what he wrote: "First, I believe the Messiah would appear after the death of Ariel Sharon. Second, the Messiah's

name is Yeshua. He is Jesus." The Jews were upset. He wrote that Jesus came and visited him and said, "I am coming."

Jesus is coming! Jesus is coming! Proclaim the Gospel to all who are unprepared for this coming. Genesis has given us the clues to these final events. He told us not to be ignorant and unprepared. Yes, Jesus is coming as a thief in the night. But we are not to be surprised. The thief told us when He was coming. He comes as a surprise to the unprepared and the lost in this world.

The early Church greeted each other with the word "Maranatha." This word means, "Even so, come quickly Lord Jesus!" (1 Corinthians 16:22). So I say to all, "Maranatha." I hope to meet you in the place God has prepared for His saints in heaven.

ENDNOTES

1 https://www.sisd.net/cms/lib/TX01001452/Centricity/Domain/1297/The_history_of_the_atom_Notes-_condensed.pdf.

2 https://www.washingtonpost.com/news/worldviews/wp/2014/10/28/pope-francis-backs-theory-of-evolution-says-god-is-no-wizard/.

3 https://www.thetrumpet.com/trumpet_issues/173.

4 https://www.livius.org/articles/place/babylon/etemenanki/.

5 Hunt, Dave, *A Woman Rides the Beast: the Roman Catholic Church and the Last Days*, p. 580, 1994.

6 https://www.christianstogether.net/Articles/319656/Christians_Together_in/Christian_Life/Christians_and_Politics/EU_architect_would.aspx.

7 www.theguardian.com/world/2016/jul/08/brexit-causes-resurgence-in-pro-eu-leanings-across-continent.

8 Douglas, J.D. (Ed.), The Illustrated Bible Dictionary, Part 1, Tyndale House Publishers, Illinois, p. 155, 1980.

9 https://www.npr.org/sections/parallels/2013/05/29/187009384/Pope-Francis-Even-Atheists-Can-Be-Redeemed.

10 https://www.christianpost.com/news/erlcs-russell-moore-takes-heat-sbc-supporting-religious-freedom-muslims-build-mosque.html.

11 Friedman, Richard Elliott, Commentary on the Torah. New York, NY: HarperCollins. p. 85, 2001.

www.ingramcontent.com/pod-product-compliance
Lightning Source LLC
Chambersburg PA
CBHW070944080526
44587CB00015B/2217